Pars

USBORNE
POLITICS
FOR BEGINNERS

Written by
Alex Frith,
Rosie Hore and
Louie Stowell

Illustrated by
Kellan Stover

Politics experts:
Dr. Hugo Drochon
Dr. Daniel Viehoff

 # Contents

Chapter 6: Big questions

Sometimes what matters most isn't who's in charge, or what they stand for, but what they're actually going to do to fix the world's problems...

Politics is boring!

Yeah, we don't care about politics!

Do you actually know what 'politics' means?

My gran told me it's not polite to talk about politics.

Turn the page to find out what politics is all about, and why it's really important to get people talking about it!

What is politics?

People often use the word politics to talk about who runs the country and how. But 'politics' actually covers the way people make decisions about how to work together in all kinds of groups, big or small.

Here's an example of a (smallish) group: a sports team.

The group has some common aims...

...but not everyone agrees on how to achieve those aims.

The group may not always agree, but they need to work together, because they want to do well.

Groups deciding the best way to work together is what politics is all about.

Most groups have a way of organizing themselves, so decisions get made in the same way each time.

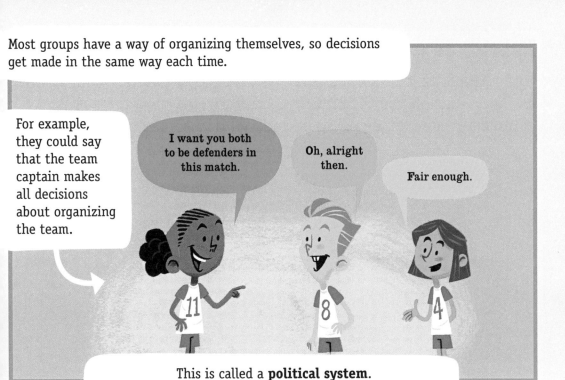

For example, they could say that the team captain makes all decisions about organizing the team.

I want you both to be defenders in this match.

Oh, alright then.

Fair enough.

This is called a **political system**.

Sometimes, people in the group will want to change the system.

I want to keep being the captain.

No, it's my turn!

Why do we have to have a captain anyway?

That's politics too.

Groups such as sports teams can be described as **societies**. In societies, not everyone can get their own way all the time. They have to have a system so that they can make decisions and get along. That's why politics is so useful.

Politics is everywhere

When people talk about politics, they're usually talking about *large societies*, such as entire countries. In those societies, the word politics can refer to almost any aspect of day-to-day life.

What should people learn in school?

Should school be optional?

Should we do business with enemy countries?

Education

Are teachers paid enough?

Foreign policy

Should school be free? What about university?

Should everyone have to learn a foreign language?

Is it always good to give aid to other countries?

Should we ever go to war?

Who should pay for doctors and hospitals?

Who's in charge of caring for the elderly?

War

Health and welfare

Should going to the dentist be free?

What should the army do when there's no war?

Might it do more good to tackle poverty first and healthcare second?

Should people pay more tax if they have a car?

Should we fly in food from other countries?

How many wind farms should we build?

Should we combat climate change, even if it hurts the economy?

Environment

Should we pay people to use less electricity?

Should we have to pay for plastic bags?

Should we give money to people who don't have a job?

Should parents all get time off work during school holidays?

How old should you be to drive?

Should bus rides be free for kids?

How much is a fair wage?

Work

At what age should people stop working?

Transport

Do we need people from other countries to move here and work?

Does our city need a new airport?

Should wearing a cycle helmet be compulsory?

Who should be allowed to borrow money from a bank?

What's the best way to help people who are homeless?

Is our society too unequal?

Is renting a flat too expensive?

How much tax should people pay?

Economy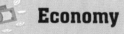

Housing

Should governments control how much things cost?

What's the best way to make people better off?

Who should be in charge of building houses?

Do we have enough homes?

Should newspapers be allowed to publish whatever they want?

Who gets to choose what's shown on TV?

Should police officers carry guns?

Is it fair to make smoking illegal?

Should museums be free to all visitors?

Culture

Law and order

Who should be allowed to get married?

How can we get more young people playing sports?

Do we want more tourists to visit us?

Who decides how long a prison sentence should be?

Who's in charge?

'Who's in charge?' is one of the biggest political questions in large societies. The answer is important, because whoever's in charge gets to tell everyone what to do. You don't always have to do what someone else tells you to, but it's hard to say 'no' to people who have *power* or *authority*.

A person with *power* can force you to do things by making you scared.

A person with *authority* doesn't have to force you, usually because you're part of a bigger group that has already agreed that he or she is allowed to tell you what to do.

Who has authority?

In a fair society, the people in charge need to have authority, not just power. The political system will only work if most people agree that those in charge are *allowed* to tell everyone what to do.

Think about all the people who might tell you what to do.
How many of those actually have authority? What do you think?

What is a government?

In a big society such as a country, the answer to the question, 'Who's in charge?' is usually: the government. The government can be a single person or a group of people, but it nearly always has the final say in decisions about how the society is run.

All governments are different. For example...

Until the end of the 1700s, France was ruled by a **king**. People believed that the king's authority came from God.

In the Middle Ages, the town of Siena in Italy was ruled by a **council** of business people which changed every two months.

In Ancient Sparta, there were **two kings** from two different royal families.

The Luba Kingdom in Central Africa was ruled by lots of **chieftains** and **one king**.

The people in a government need to have authority if they're going to tell everyone what to do, and trust that people will accept it. But where does a government's authority come from? It could come from tradition, a *higher* authority, a popularity contest, or perhaps it's a choice based on wisdom...

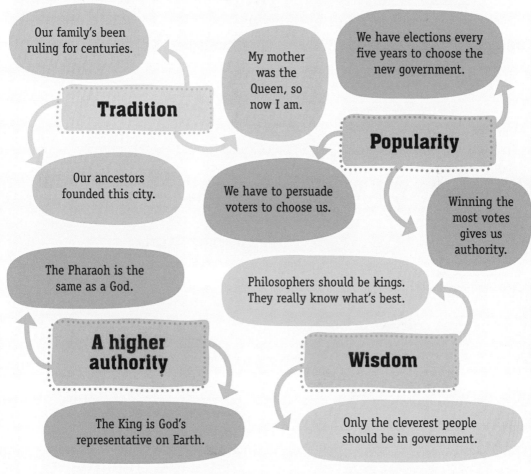

Our family's been ruling for centuries.

Tradition

My mother was the Queen, so now I am.

We have elections every five years to choose the new government.

Popularity

Our ancestors founded this city.

We have to persuade voters to choose us.

Winning the most votes gives us authority.

The Pharaoh is the same as a God.

Philosophers should be kings. They really know what's best.

A higher authority

Wisdom

The King is God's representative on Earth.

Only the cleverest people should be in government.

If a government is claiming to have authority, it needs to have a good reason – and that reason needs to be accepted by most (if not all) of the people in society. A government with both those things is known as a **legitimate government**.

Democracy isn't working! The people in my country keep voting for the wrong person to be in charge. Grr!

Sometimes, people *don't* accept that the current government is legitimate, and want a change. They might protest, demand reforms, or start a revolution – which could lead to a *new* government.

Chapter 1:
All kinds of governments

Throughout history, people have argued about what kind of government is best for their societies. Governments have changed too – either gradually over time, or suddenly when one group of people decides they've had enough of the current type of government.

This chapter will explain some of the different kinds of governments in the past – from the very beginning of something called **democracy** in Ancient Greece, to rebels in America who helped to elect the first President of the United States.

Ancient democracy

When the city of Athens in Greece was first founded, it was ruled by the wealthiest people who lived there; other Athenians had no say. Around 2,700 years ago, people demanded changes so they could rule themselves. This was the beginning of the world's first **democracy**.

Anyone who was a citizen could take part in government. But who was a citizen?

I'm a citizen!

Sorry, but you're not. Women can't be citizens.

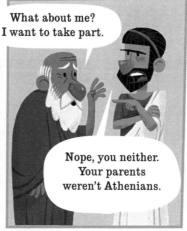

What about me? I want to take part.

Nope, you neither. Your parents weren't Athenians.

I'm an Athenian!

Definitely not! Slaves can't be citizens.

In Greek, the word *democracy* means 'rule of the people'. But citizens had to be free men, over 20 years old, and both parents had to be born in Athens. This meant only 10-20% of the people who lived in Athens were citizens.

The political system was made up of two main bodies: the **Boule** (or Council) and the **Ecclesia** (or Assembly).

Citizens
(around 6,000 men)

Boule

500 members, chosen by random draw

- decides when the Ecclesia meets
- decides what will be discussed
- comes up with new laws

Ecclesia

All citizens encouraged to attend

- discusses big issues
- accepts or rejects the laws decided on by the boule

This is how a session in the Ecclesia might have looked, during a debate on whether Athens should go to war.

Everyone who attended the Ecclesia had the chance to speak. It didn't matter who you were (although men over 50 were allowed to go first, so it did matter a *bit*).

People who were persuasive speakers were known as **orators**.

Oi, whippersnapper! My turn first.

Fellow Athenians, do not vote for war.

Speaker's platform

The Assembly met on Pnyx Hill. *Pnyx* is the Greek word for 'tightly packed together.'

Speeches were timed so they didn't go over about six minutes.

Look at those two idiots!

You're late!

Politics is boring.

Citizens had a duty to attend the Assembly. Guards used a rope covered in red paint to hurry latecomers along. If you got red on your clothes, it showed you weren't a very good citizen.

The word 'idiot' comes from the Greek word *idiotes*, which means 'private citizen'. It was used as an insult for someone who wasn't interested in politics.

The Roman Republic

Meanwhile, in Italy, Rome was becoming a great city, ruled by kings. In 509BC, wealthy families, known as **patricians**, rebelled against the latest king. They set up a new form of government, called a **republic**, which means a government without a king or queen.

In the king's place, the patricians chose two **consuls** to do the job of ruling Rome.

The consuls' power was limited by...

Consuls
Having two meant that neither one got too powerful.

The Senate
This was a body of patricians who advised the consuls.

Tribunes
These were representatives of the ordinary citizens, known as **plebians**.

The three parts were linked to make sure that no person or group had too much of the power.

This is sometimes known as a system of **checks and balances**. It means each part of government has its power limited by the other parts.

Dictatorship

In an emergency – such as a rebellion, invasion or war – the Republic had special rules in place. The Roman people could elect a **dictator**: someone who could temporarily rule however he liked, with no checks from the Senate or Tribunes.

Cincinnatus was a dictator twice in his life.

He's regarded as the ideal example of how the emergency rule can work...

Cincinnatus had been a wise consul...

It's not a bad life.

...but moved out of Rome to become a farmer.

Years later...

Cincinnatus! Rome is under attack!

The Senate have appointed you dictator.

See you in a while, Taurus.

Cincinnatus led the army...

For Rome! For glory!

...and won the war.

16 days later, he was back at the farm.

Done and dusted.

But dictatorship didn't always go to plan. The last dictator of Rome was Julius Caesar, who refused to step down. He made himself dictator for life (cut short by an assassination plot). Today, dictatorship is almost always seen as a bad thing.

Empires and emperors

The Romans became more and more powerful, conquering land beyond Rome and building up an empire under Roman control. But in Rome itself, the system began to collapse, and in 27BC, the republic was replaced by rule under an emperor.

The land the emperor controlled grew until it covered much of Europe. This is how it looked at its biggest, 1,800 years ago.

The Roman Empire was split into regions known as **provinces**. Roman officials known as governors were assigned to each province.

The emperor ruled from Rome and had complete authority. His 'decrees' – public pronouncements – automatically became law.

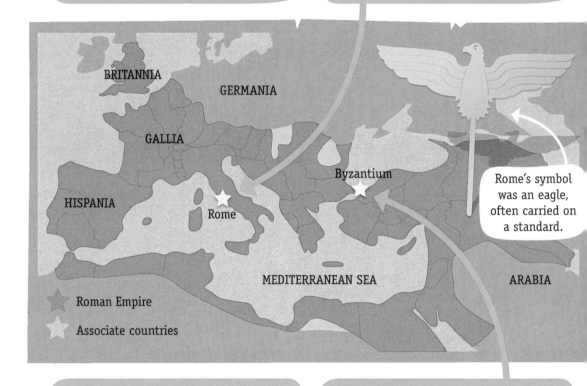

BRITANNIA

GERMANIA

GALLIA

HISPANIA

Byzantium

Rome

Rome's symbol was an eagle, often carried on a standard.

⭐ Roman Empire

⭐ Associate countries

MEDITERRANEAN SEA

ARABIA

People living in the provinces outside of Rome itself had to pay taxes to the emperor, but actually they had quite a lot of freedom to live their lives.

The Roman army protected the empire's borders, and conquered ever more land. Eventually, the empire got so big, it was impossible to rule from Rome. In 285, it was split into two, ruled by two emperors in two different cities.

The Roman government was in charge of a huge area and a huge number of people, many more than most governments today. This is how they did it...

There are 30 legions stationed around the Empire, with 5,000 men in each. People are scared of us, and that keeps them in line.

Army general

I'm building a new city, with modern sewers *and* a sports arena. When people see how cool it is, they won't want to complain about Roman rule.

Architect

I served in the Roman army for years. I was rewarded with a Roman citizenship. Made me feel pretty special!

Ex-soldier living near Rome

The Romans still let me make decisions about local things, so I guess I can live with that.

Local chief

I used to be a Roman soldier. They gave me and my family a plot of land in this province when I retired.

We show the locals how great Roman culture is...

...and we can let the emperor know if anyone causes trouble.

Roman family in the outer provinces

China: from empire to meritocracy

Meanwhile, large parts of Asia were ruled by an emperor, too. Emperors often gained power through military might, but the actual work of government was done by highly trained people called **civil servants**. From the 7th century, civil servants were chosen by exam. Only the very best passed the exams – this system is known as a **meritocracy**.

If you wanted to be a government official, you had to study for years at university.

Just off to my four hour calligraphy class.

The exams were fiendish. Only 1 in 3,000 people passed...

...and cheating was punished with death.

Those who passed were given a junior job in government. To get to the very top, they had to pass *nine more* exams.

My brain is going to explode!

In Europe, before the 19th century, people got government jobs if they were members of ruling families, a system known as **nepotism**. But the Chinese system eventually inspired European governments to give people jobs based on merit instead. But meritocracy has its own problems...

Pah! What problems? We want talented people to rule.

It's ok for you. I'm too poor to afford education, so I've got no chance, however talented I am.

I'm not great at exams, but I might be really good at the job.

What use is a load of geeks in government? We want people with **VISION**!

Feudalism

In 1066, a ruler named Harold was crowned king of England. But a rival, William of Normandy (in France), thought *he* should be king. So he sailed to England, fought and killed Harold, and took the crown for himself. He earned the nickname 'William the Conqueror'.

William had to find a way to rule England, a foreign country where no one had any reason to be loyal to him. His answer was **feudalism**. This was a version of **monarchy** – rule by king or queen – that continued in England for hundreds of years. This is how it worked:

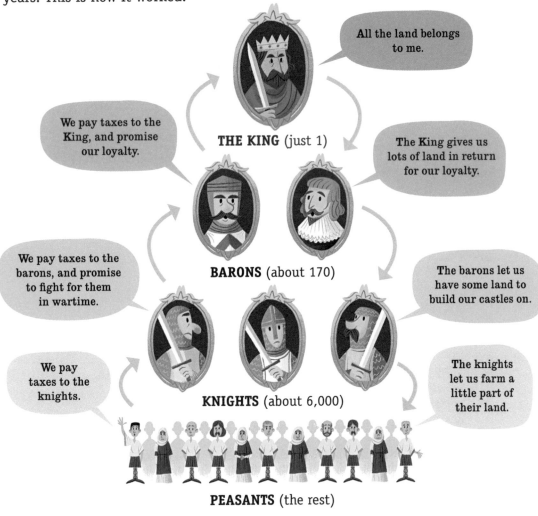

All the land belongs to me.

THE KING (just 1)

We pay taxes to the King, and promise our loyalty.

The King gives us lots of land in return for our loyalty.

BARONS (about 170)

We pay taxes to the barons, and promise to fight for them in wartime.

The barons let us have some land to build our castles on.

We pay taxes to the knights.

The knights let us farm a little part of their land.

KNIGHTS (about 6,000)

PEASANTS (the rest)

This system sounds quite peaceful, if unfair on the peasants. But in fact, some people tried to rebel against William. His power as king had no limits – so he could get away with whatever he wanted, and often used violence to control any rebels.

Absolute monarchy

Absolute monarchy or **absolutism** describes a government where all of the power is in the hands of a king or queen, a style of politics common in 17th and 18th century Europe. One of the most famous absolute monarchs was King Louis XIV of France (1643-1715). He used all kinds of tricks to hold onto as much power as he could.

My methods achieve *absolutely* fabulous results!

War glory

Louis spent lots of money making France's army the strongest and most modern in Europe, and sent them to fight his enemies so he could secure France's borders.

Image

Louis built a grand palace, and commissioned portraits that made him look like a powerful ruler.

Money

Louis updated France's tax system so that more money went straight to him.

Intimidation

Louis used his power to crush his opponents within France, especially people who disagreed with his Catholic faith.

Loyal advisors

In the past, the king's advisors came from *noble* families – rich and powerful people. Instead, Louis hired less wealthy people. That meant they relied on the king for their position in society, so were less likely to disagree with him.

Divine justification

When Louis was born, his parents had been trying to have a baby for 23 years. So people thought he was a gift from God, and Louis believed it too. He claimed that God had given him the right to rule.

Centralization

Before Louis, remote places in France often had their own laws and tax systems. Louis brought the whole country under the control of the central government.

Controlling the nobles

Louis' biggest problem was to see off challenges from France's noble families. Powerful nobles had rebelled against Louis' father, and there were riots in Paris. Louis needed to find a way to stop these nobles from getting too powerful, or too likely to rebel against him. So, he ordered the troublesome ones to come to live at his palace in Versailles, where he could control their lives.

The nobles had to attend to him from morning...

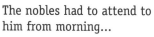

Your tea, my lord.

...till night.

Your bedtime story, your majesty.

Hmph. No time to scheme.

He also made life at court very expensive...

Here's the dress code for this season.

10 fancy-dress balls in the next month! I can't afford it!

Many nobles got into debt, and had to ask Louis for money. This made them dependent on him. Besides having no time to plot against him, they couldn't afford to, either.

Keep your friends close, and your enemies poor, I say!

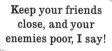

Please?

Please?

Can we borrow just a little?

Self-government

Around 300 years ago, the government in Britain controlled colonies on the east coast of North America. In the 1770s, one influential group of people who lived there, known as **Patriots**, argued this was unfair. They began demanding the right to govern themselves.

In 1773, the British changed how tea was taxed, without asking American colonists. This led to an act of rebellion known today as the 'Boston Tea Party'.

1773. Boston. A shipment of tea arrives from Britain...

Patriots storm the ship and throw 342 chests overboard.

The British demand payment, but the Patriots refuse.

No taxation without representation!

Britain controlled 13 regions, known today as *states*. After the Boston Tea Party, Patriots in each state started making their own alternative governments, and refused to obey British rules. The 13 states declared themselves independent from Britain in 1776, and the **War of Independence** began.

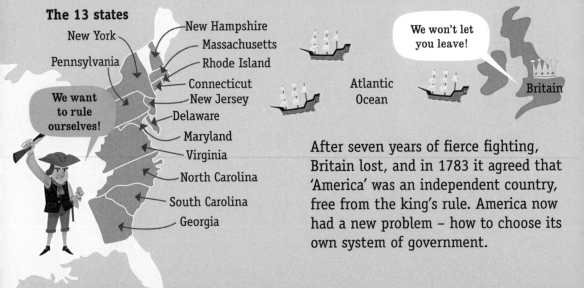

The 13 states

New York
Pennsylvania
New Hampshire
Massachusetts
Rhode Island
Connecticut
New Jersey
Delaware
Maryland
Virginia
North Carolina
South Carolina
Georgia

We want to rule ourselves!

We won't let you leave!

Britain

Atlantic Ocean

After seven years of fierce fighting, Britain lost, and in 1783 it agreed that 'America' was an independent country, free from the king's rule. America now had a new problem – how to choose its own system of government.

A new constitution

During the war, each state had its own **constitution**, which was a set of rules to organize how their state government would be run.

In 1787, representatives from the thirteen states, known as the **Founding Fathers**, met in Philadelphia, Pennsylvania, to discuss a new constitution for a *national* government for their new nation, the **United States of America**. Here are three of the Fathers, who took inspiration from three systems:

We should be a **republic**, like Ancient Rome. Everyone should be able to elect representatives to serve in government.

We should have a group of elected politicians called a **parliament**, as the British do.

We must follow our **Declaration of Independence**. We stated that all men are created equal – as French philosophers have proved.

James Madison   Alexander Hamilton   Benjamin Franklin

In 1788, the Founding Fathers combined these ideas and agreed their new constitution. In 1789, after lots of arguing, they added a list of ten amendments, written in a document known as the **Bill of Rights**.

Look at me! I'm *perfect*.

OK, *now* I'm perfect...

...sort of.

The **Constitution** said there should be an elected president, appointed judges and a House of Representatives and Senate. See more on page 42.

The **Bill of Rights** made sure the rights of individual people – and the states – were respected, unless those people were slaves, or Native Americans...

Representative democracy

The United States' new constitution created a system of government called **representative democracy**. But it wasn't very similar to how democracy had looked when it first started, in ancient Athens.

> I'm a citizen. I vote directly on political questions.

> I'm a citizen, too. I vote for members of Congress, and *they* vote directly on questions as my **representatives**.

Ancient Athens
(Direct democracy)

USA
(Representative democracy)

America was a much bigger and more complicated society than Athens, so direct democracy would have been very difficult to organize.

But there was a more fundamental reason too. One of the Founding Fathers, John Adams, called it...

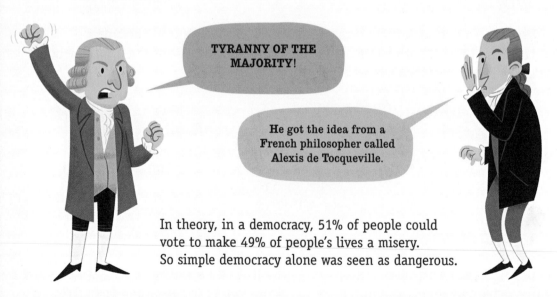

> TYRANNY OF THE MAJORITY!

> He got the idea from a French philosopher called Alexis de Tocqueville.

In theory, in a democracy, 51% of people could vote to make 49% of people's lives a misery. So simple democracy alone was seen as dangerous.

To prevent a tyranny of the majority, the American constitution created several branches of government, and included checks and balances – just as the Roman Republic had done. To read more about the American system, see pages 42-43.

Most countries in the world today are representative democracies (although they have differences between them). Here are some of the reasons for preferring representative democracy to direct democracy.

Because people don't have time to make every decision themselves.

Because it would be too slow and expensive for every person to vote on every issue.

Because representatives are often experts at something that they need to understand.

Because most of us don't *want* to be involved in every decision.

The perfect representative?

You might not know who they are, but you probably have representatives. You could think of them a little like a servant you've sent to buy you things you need from a shopping list...

...but many people – including the Founding Fathers – said representatives ought to do *more*. They should be wise enough to make decisions for you *better* than you can yourself. That's the theory, anyway...

VOTE FOR ME

Chapter 2:
Political systems

A **political system** is a set of basic rules about government, such as who gets to be in charge, how they are chosen, and how a government divides up its many responsibilities. Most systems are designed to hold together a **state** – the word for an independent country with its own government.

No country has a perfect political system. Sometimes, arguments about how to change the system have led to wars and revolutions. And some people think it'd be better to do away with government altogether.

Types of political systems

In your life, you deal with all sorts of different political systems, even if people don't describe them like that.

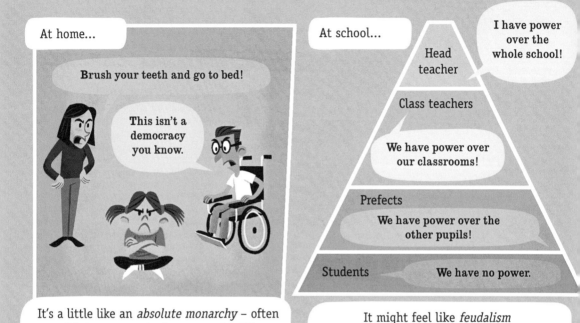

At home...

Brush your teeth and go to bed!

This isn't a democracy you know.

It's a little like an *absolute monarchy* – often with two monarchs (see pages 22-23).

At school...

I have power over the whole school!

Head teacher

Class teachers

We have power over our classrooms!

Prefects

We have power over the other pupils!

Students

We have no power.

It might feel like *feudalism* (see page 21).

At times, it can feel as if there's no system in place at all...

That's my money!

But I found it.

But it fell out of my pocket!

Finders keepers, losers weepers.

I'm telling!

What are you, 7?

What shall we do?

I don't mind.

Whatever you like.

I really don't mind.

You choose.

No, you!

Argh! No wonder we never have any fun.

Creating a system

Most states are made up of different groups of people. So, systems have to balance the need to be fair to each group with the need to keep everything running smoothly. Some systems were invented by giving very different answers to some basic questions.

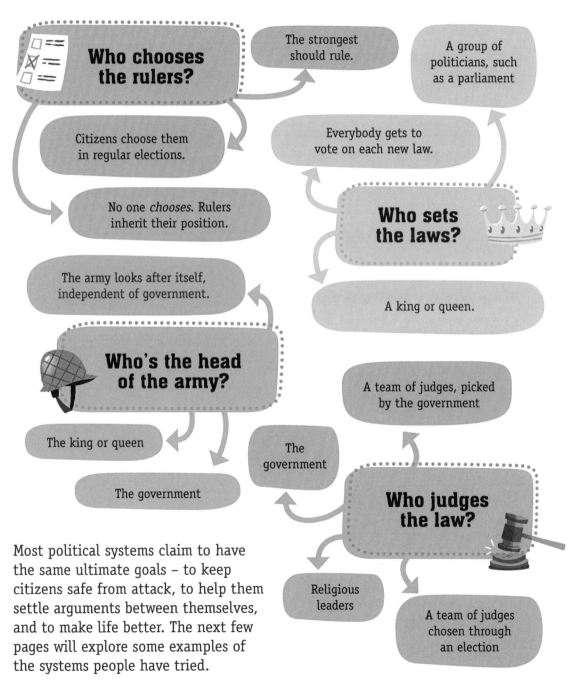

Who chooses the rulers?

The strongest should rule.

A group of politicians, such as a parliament

Citizens choose them in regular elections.

Everybody gets to vote on each new law.

No one *chooses*. Rulers inherit their position.

Who sets the laws?

The army looks after itself, independent of government.

A king or queen.

Who's the head of the army?

A team of judges, picked by the government

The king or queen

The government

The government

Who judges the law?

Religious leaders

A team of judges chosen through an election

Most political systems claim to have the same ultimate goals – to keep citizens safe from attack, to help them settle arguments between themselves, and to make life better. The next few pages will explore some examples of the systems people have tried.

Authoritarian systems

Until the 1800s, most states were ruled by a single very powerful leader. Today, states with this kind of government – either a single person called a **dictator**, or a small committee – are known as **authoritarian** states. These leaders have power to make their own laws, often designed to help them keep power. Here are some examples:

No opposition

Many dictators came to power after an election. It suits them to pretend they still run a democratic country – but they don't want to lose any future elections, so they set new rules to make sure no one else can win.

Watch everyone

Some authoritarian leaders employ huge numbers of spies, to watch and listen to everyone around them – and report back to the leader.

Control the media

All TV, radio and even internet broadcasts must be approved by a state **censor** – someone who can remove any stories that the leader doesn't want citizens to know about.

No gatherings

National police are allowed to disperse any public gatherings of groups larger than a family – to prevent people from plotting a revolution.

The strictest dictators use laws to demand total obedience, and even hero worship, from their citizens. States with these laws in place are described as **totalitarian**.

No criticism

Anyone who speaks or publishes ideas that criticize the leader, or the state as a whole, can be arrested and imprisoned.

Gulp

CLAP CLAP

Kim Jong-un inherited his father's role as Supreme Leader of North Korea in 2014. This country is often described as a totalitarian state.

Army rule

Sometimes, a country's military chiefs seize power. These chiefs may decide to stay in charge until they feel the country is ready for an election – which may take decades.

A government controlled by the army is often known as a **military junta**.

Argentina was governed by a series of different military juntas five times between 1930 and 1983.

God's law

In some countries, spiritual and religious leaders are in charge. They often have support from huge numbers of people, more than any army.

A political system based on religious laws is known as a **theocracy**. These laws can be as strict as any dictator's laws.

In Iran in 1979, devout Muslims deposed the government and declared their spiritual leader, Ayatollah Khomeini, to be the new ruler.

Fascist dictators

One political movement, known as **fascism**, grew popular by appealing to people's love of their country. But they did it by preaching hate for foreigners, and bullying people into voting for them.

The world's first fascist party was founded by Benito Mussolini in Italy in 1919. In 1922, he was elected as prime minister. In 1925, he declared himself dictator.

Communism

During the 20th century, several countries tried to set up a new system known as **communism**. In theory, it required everyone to share possessions – food, clothing, housing – equally. In reality, although communist governments brought about great changes, none managed to set up a perfectly equal society.

The key ideas of communism were developed by a German philosopher named Karl Marx, in his book *The Communist Manifesto*, published in 1848.

The system we live in is unfair! Most people – the *workers* – do all the work. Only a few people – *capitalists* – exploit the workers to get all the money.

One day, the workers will fight and overthrow those wicked capitalists!

During the 20th century, determined leaders in several countries gathered people who were inspired by Marx's ideas. Each helped overthrow an existing government, often an authoritarian one, and worked to set up a communist state.

Lenin (Russia)
Chairman of the Council of the People's Commissars
1917-1924

Mao Zedong (China)
Chairman of the Communist Party
1949-1976

Fidel Castro (Cuba)
First Secretary of the Communist Party
1961-2011

Ho Chi Minh (Vietnam)
Chairman of the Communist Party
1945-1969

Class war

Marx and others described European societies as being made up of groups called **classes**. Monarchs and lords were the *upper class*. People who owned factories or had well-paid jobs were the *middle class*.

Communism was intended as a system to fight for the rights of the *working class* – people who did most of the work, but were paid very little.

Political leaders such as Lenin gained great support from the working class.

Flag of the *Soviets* – Russian communists

A sickle for farmers

A hammer for factory workers

By gathering and protesting in massive numbers, communists were able to imprison, execute or banish most of the upper class.

New leaders – people who championed the working class (but were often themselves from the middle class) – took over.

Houses previously owned by wealthy, upper class individuals were now taken over by the government.

Middle and working class people couldn't sell their wares – instead, they gave everything to the government...

...who then shared it around.

The system relied on people working hard, and not cheating. But when times were hard, people *did* cheat.

Communist leaders had to cope with famine and war. To try to make their system work, they used exactly the same tactics as totalitarian dictators, and often carried them out even more ruthlessly...

Didn't we help this guy overthrow the old system? How is the new system better?

Shh! Don't badmouth our leader – you'll get arrested...

Rule of empire

For much of the 19th and 20th centuries, many European countries invaded other countries around the world, creating giant nations known as **empires**. The countries they conquered didn't have their own governments, and were known as **colonies** or **dependencies**.

This map shows some of the European colonies around the world, in the early 20th century.

NORTH AMERICA

EUROPE

ASIA

Pacific Ocean

Atlantic Ocean

Pacific Ocean

AFRICA

Indian Ocean

SOUTH AMERICA

AUSTRALIA

- Belgium
- Denmark
- France
- Germany
- Britain
- Italy
- Netherlands
- Portugal
- Spain

Empires used different systems to keep control in their colonies, such as:

Direct rule

The ruling nation imposed its own system of government on the country.

For example, the main government in France ruled all French colonies.

Indirect rule

The ruling nation hand-picked locals to be in charge of their country – as long as they did as they were told.

For example, the British Empire in India

Settler rule

Europeans moved into the colonies and formed their own governments, with no input from locals.

For example, British settlers in South Africa

Empires and violence

Europeans often built up their empires by military conquest, and ruled in an authoritarian way. They believed their way of life was superior to the ones they encountered in their colonies, and even believed it was their duty to 'civilize' the people they met. But mostly they wanted to make money from crops or mineral treasures in each colony, and to gain power to compete with other empires.

Empires used a variety of methods to keep power in their colonies.

Language and religion

All government business was conducted in the language of the ruling empire, making it hard to overturn the system from within.

Often, people were forced to adopt the empire's culture, too, for example by converting to a new religion.

A is for APPLE

Border confusion

Empires made treaties with each other – and not with locals – to draw up borders. Communities living on both sides of the new borders were split apart.

Seizing land

Rich settlers took control of the best land, so they could make money for themselves – and keep locals from getting rich from their own resources.

Making new enemies

Ruling governments sometimes appointed local leaders from minority groups. These minorities often ended up being hated by rival groups.

Taxation without benefits

Most colonies had to pay taxes to the ruling government. Often, these taxes were spent in other parts of the empire, taking money away from the colony itself.

The end of the empires

During the 20th century, many colonies successfully campaigned and fought for independence. Meanwhile, countries around the world began to agree that empires were not a legitimate form of government. However, many former colonies are still struggling with the after-effects of colonization. Find out more on pages 75, 90, and 101.

The democratic process

Most countries today are **democracies**. Just as in ancient Athens, a democratic political system is designed to let citizens influence the way their country is run. Here's how it works in the most common version, known as **representative democracy**.

Citizens

(Everyone who is allowed to vote – find out more in chapter 3)

Everyone gets to vote for a representative in a contest, called an **election**.

Elected representatives*

You chose *us* to do the work so *you* don't have to!

In government, groups of elected representatives get together to debate policy ideas...

The media

(internet, TV, radio, newspapers)

News outlets explain the debates, and hire experts to give their opinions on new policies and bills.

...and turn them into proposals for new laws, called **bills**.

Many news sources try to sound neutral. But in fact, each has its own **bias** – when people mix facts with opinions.

Today, the government debated a new tax to *protect the environment.*

Today, the government debated a new tax to *charge car drivers.*

Citizens

People react to the news in different ways, creating something called **public opinion**. Of course, there's usually more than one opinion...

Elected representatives

Representatives often react to public opinion (and the media) before they vote to turn a bill into a new law. If they ignore all opinions, or side with an unpopular one, they may lose their jobs at the next election.

I'm angry!

I'm pleased!

*in the UK, they're called MPs.

Sometimes, governments decide that a decision is so important – or has so many supporters on opposite sides – that they ask everyone to vote on it. This is known as a **referendum**.

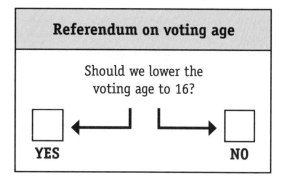

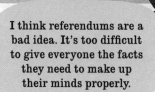

I think referendums are a bad idea. It's too difficult to give everyone the facts they need to make up their minds properly.

You're just saying that because the vote didn't go the way you wanted it to!

Some smaller countries, such as Switzerland, hold referendums for lots of decisions. The Swiss system is a modern example of **direct democracy**.

Majority rules

Many democracies use a simple system: whoever or whatever gets the most votes wins. This is called a **majority**. But sometimes, the majority winner might not actually be what *most people* want. For example...

We can buy one tub of ice cream to share. What should we get?

Vanilla

Strawberry

Chocolate

Bubblegum!!

Two votes for vanilla, so vanilla wins.

Yesss!

But more of us wanted anything *but* vanilla!

You can find out more about voting and elections in chapter 3.

Sharing power

Representatives have to work together to make all kinds of decisions. To prevent any one person from having too much power, most democracies split up the government's responsibilities across three groups, often called **branches**.

Executive branch

Carries out – or **executes** – policies and laws.

It's often a single person, such as a **president** or **prime minister**, with the help of a group called a **cabinet**.

The executive branch usually has to approve any new laws, and can often propose them – but it can't *create* them. That's the job of the legislative branch...

Legislative branch

Makes new laws and gets rid of old laws (called **legislation**), and discusses **policies** – ideas for how to make society work.

The legislative branch is usually made up of elected representatives, split into groups known as **political parties**. People in rival parties often disagree with each other.

Judicial branch

Makes sure the other two branches aren't breaking any rules, especially rules from a national constitution.

Ensures that everyone in the country, including the leader, obeys the same set of laws, or faces the same punishments.

Usually made up of a small group of **judges** – expert lawyers – who are appointed, not elected.

How the three branches work together

In the legislative branch, new laws are debated...

There's too much litter! Someone suggested making a law to stop manufacturers using too much packaging. Let's debate whether that's a good idea.

This is a great idea because...

Who will benefit?

This is a terrible idea because...

Let's have a trial run.

question

This part of the process is what people often think of when they hear the word 'politics'.

debate

I agree!

Is this what most people actually want?

argue

Can you give us some evidence?

grumble

It doesn't sound very practical.

After the debate, there's a vote...

Yes

No

All those in favour?

In the executive branch, laws are put into action...

Cabinet

OK, I'll sign the new law to make it official.

And we'll put it into practice.

In the judicial branch...

We've had complaints from manufacturers!

We're going to check that the new law doesn't go against their rights.

This is the part that makes sure no one person, or branch of government, can do whatever it likes.

Democracy in the USA

One of the world's most famous political systems is the one used by the United States of America. Authority is shared between three sections: a leader, called the **President**, and two groups of representatives called **Congress** and the **Supreme Court**.

What the President does

- responsible for ensuring that laws and policies are put into practice, and appoints a Cabinet to help with this.
- appoints new judges to the Supreme Court.
- in charge of the armed forces.
- can approve – or refuse – new laws.

The President is chosen by an election every four years, voted for by everyone* in the country. Currently, presidents can only serve two terms.

The President and Cabinet work in the White House, in America's capital city, Washington, D.C.

What Congress does

- suggests, debates and – if enough people agree – can send new laws to the President for approval.
- divides other areas of responsibility between two separate groups, called the **House of Representatives** (or **House** for short), and the **Senate**.

The House is responsible for setting up new taxes, or suggesting changes to old tax laws.

The Senate is in charge of approving people the President picks for the Cabinet (and other jobs), and makes agreements with other countries.

All members of Congress are chosen by elections within their separate states.

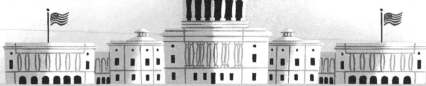

Both groups meet in the Capitol Building, also in Washington, D.C.

*Not quite everyone. Find out more on page 60.

What the Supreme Court does

Decides whether or not new laws might go against the Constitution (see page 25).

Led by a judge called the **Chief Justice**, and up to eight Associate Justices. New Justices are appointed by the President whenever there is a vacancy.

We also have the authority to overturn decisions made by courts across the **US**.

This is the Supreme Court Building, also in Washington, D.C. In most countries, government buildings are in the capital city.

(Not) Getting things done

For 250 years, America's system of checks and balances has – so far – helped prevent any one person from abusing his or her power. But the same system can sometimes make it difficult to make *any* changes.

I want to improve our healthcare system.

We'll draft you a Bill to take to Congress.

And we'll try to persuade Representatives and Senators to vote for the Bill.

People from Congress on the President's side

We don't like your Bill.

We'll persuade Representatives and Senators to vote against the Bill until you change it to something we agree with.

But the new law isn't what I really wanted now! I refuse to approve it.

People from Congress not on the President's side

Democracy in the UK

The UK is officially ruled by a monarch – the *executive* – but real political power belongs to the *legislative* branch, known as **Parliament**. A similar system is used in many countries, such as Canada, Australia, Spain, Norway, Sweden and Japan. Here's how it works in the UK:

Monarch

A king or queen calls on Parliament to meet – but doesn't actually have any say in what happens there.

Houses of Parliament

Two groups of people, called **Houses**, meet to debate and vote on new laws.

House of Lords

Over 1,000 people, known as **Lords**, can suggest amendments to laws, and can vote against laws passed by the Commons. Most lords are chosen by MPs, and none are elected.

House of Commons

650 **Members of Parliament (MPs)**, who are elected every five years. MPs debate laws. If more than half agree, they can make new laws and scrap old ones.

Government and Opposition

Most MPs belong to a political party (see page 56). If one party has more than half of the MPs, they form the **Government**.

The party with the second-most MPs is known as the **Opposition**. They argue against government ideas and stop them doing whatever they like.

Prime Minister

The leader of the political party with the most MPs becomes the **Prime Minister** – the most powerful politician in the country.

Cabinet

The Prime Minister appoints some MPs, known as **ministers**, to be responsible for different areas of government policy, such as health or education.

Inside the House of Commons

People called recorders take careful notes of everything that is said.

Speaker

An MP who runs the House, and chooses who can speak.

Front bench

The Prime Minister and other Cabinet ministers sit here.

Opposition front bench

The leader of the Opposition is in charge of challenging the Prime Minister to defend policy decisions, and help make sure he or she is running the country properly.

Back benchers

Most MPs don't have a specific role. They are supposed to vote the way their party leaders tell them (but don't always).

Independent MPs and MPs from other parties.

Ayes and Noes

When MPs vote on any new laws, they have to walk along one of two corridors, called **lobbies**, that lead behind the rows of benches on either side of the speaker.

AYES

People who vote 'yes' are counted as 'ayes to the right'.

NOES

People who vote 'no' are counted as 'noes to the left'.

Gallery

Where spectators and journalists can watch.

For most debates, only some MPs are present. MPs who live and work nearby are summoned by an electronic bell to tell them when it's time to vote.

Running a country

Governments decide how a country should be run. But putting those decisions into action is a job for non-politicians known as **civil servants**. Here's how it works in the UK.

Minister or Secretary

(A member of the cabinet with responsibility for one area, such as education)

Responsible for turning policy ideas, such as improving school attendance, into practical suggestions.

Civil servants

Write up specific ideas into a document called a *White Paper*.

We'll consult lots of education experts to get their ideas.

Civil servants

Civil servants re-draft the Paper to turn it into a *Bill of Parliament*.

Experts

A few experts help write the Paper; lots of experts read it and suggest improvements.

Parliament

MPs hold a debate about the Bill, and vote on whether or not to turn it into a new law.

Experts say we should let teenagers sleep longer. Let's vote for new school hours.

Nonsense! Teenagers need to learn discipline.

Civil servants

If the Bill becomes a law, civil servants explain the details to every school, such as...

Calling all head teachers!

At schools

New school hours will be 10am to 5pm.

Navigating the system

A system in which civil servants run the day-to-day business of government is often called a **bureaucracy**. It means, 'rule by people who sit behind desks'. Bureaucracies have strict rules about who civil servants can help, and what they can and can't do. Sometimes, navigating the system can be a slow process...

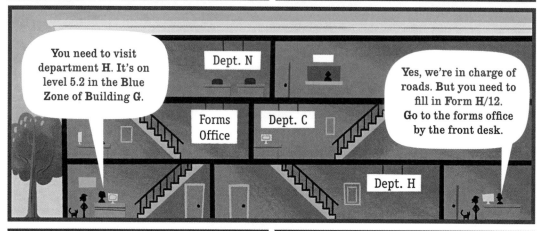

In the past, civil servants often tied bundles of papers together using red tape. Today, people often refer to 'red tape' when they're talking about the difficulty of getting help in a bureaucratic system.

Local politics

Political news is mostly about what's happening in national government. But often the things that affect people's daily lives the most have to do with their home towns or regions. This is the world of **local government**.

National government

(sometimes called central government)

- Makes laws and decisions that affect the whole country.
- Controls and spends an enormous amount of money.

Local government

- Can make laws and decisions that only affect a small area – as long as they don't go against national laws.
- Controls and spends a smaller amount of money.

Here's an example:

National government agrees rules about new building works:

RULES

- no new buildings allowed inside national conservation areas.

- all houses must meet national safety standards.

Local government approves applications for specific building projects.

This is a team of councillors, who have been elected to be part of a local government.

Do lots of local people *object* to the building?

Will the project bring more money into the local area?

Does the project plan meet national standards?

How many people *want* the building?

If you're unhappy about a local building project, you need to talk to your local government.

Federal politics

Many of the biggest countries in the world, such as the USA, Germany, Brazil and Russia, are known as **Federal Republics**.

'Federal' means a country is made up of independent states that have their own governments, who agree to follow some laws set by a national government. 'Republic' means a country has an elected leader – such as a president – instead of a monarch.

One Federal Republic, India, is the largest democracy in the world. It's home to over one billion people. Here's how each person is able to have representatives.

India is divided into 29 *states* and 7 *union territories*.

Levels of government

A president signs off laws and decisions made by a central parliament.

Parliament is made up of representatives chosen after nationwide elections.

Parliament is led by a prime minister, who leads the party with the most seats in parliament.

Jawaharlal Nehru was India's first and longest serving prime minister.

States (and most territories) have their own governments, made up of representatives chosen in state elections.

State governments collect taxes and make laws just for their state.

Most states are divided into smaller sections called *districts*, many of which have their own government, too.

Rural places are governed by groups called *Gram Panchayat*.

Within some districts there are even smaller governments...

The biggest cities are governed by *councillors*.

International politics

To avoid wars, governments from different countries often make agreements with one another, called **treaties**. Most aren't just about war – treaties can make it easier for people to move around, or trade goods, or share information. Sometimes, groups of countries go even further – forming international organizations with common aims and interests. Here are a few examples:

The United Nations (UN)

UN flag

Nearly every country in the world is part of the UN. Known as member states, they all agree to follow its rules, and to work together to help promote global goals.

People called **delegates** from each member state work in the UN Headquarters in New York City.

Interpreters translate speeches through headphones, so everyone can understand.

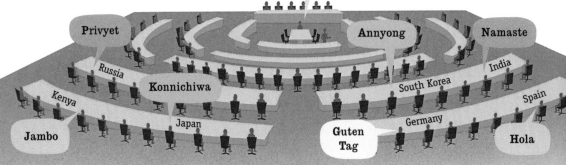

Hello everyone

Privyet

Annyong

Namaste

Russia

India

Konnichiwa

South Korea

Kenya

Spain

Jambo

Japan

Germany

Guten Tag

Hola

Global goals

- maintaining peace between countries
- protecting the environment
- promoting equality and fairness in all societies
- giving aid, such as food and shelter, to places that have suffered from natural disasters or war

Global authority

Five member states – China, France, Russia, the UK and the US – have more power than the others. They're known together as the **UN Permanent Security Council**.

If all five agree, the Council can authorize military action against a country, or impose **sanctions** – making it illegal to trade goods with that country.

The European Union (EU)

Most European states have agreed to share their resources, allowing people to live, work and trade across the Union.

EU flag

The EU has its own parliament, too, based in Brussels and Strasbourg. Citizens from each member state elect representatives to vote in the European Parliament, for example on how to spend the money each state provides.

The Arab League

An alliance between most countries in the Middle East and North Africa, to help protect each other and to share resources.

Arab League flag

North Atlantic Treaty Organization (NATO)

A military alliance between most countries in North America and Europe, who agree to help defend each other, and to share resources including weapons.

The African Union

An alliance between most countries in Africa to promote unity and peace, and to set up an international system of trade.

African Union flag

NATO flag

Homes away from home

Most governments send officials, called **ambassadors**, to live and work in foreign countries. It's their job to negotiate with the government in that country.

The ambassador for each country, and his or her team, work in a building called an **embassy**.

Although the building is in France, it's technically part of Australia.

Hello! I'm the ambassador for Australia in France.

Open up in the name of the law!

Your laws don't apply in here! I'm in Australian territory.

What if there was no system?

Some people think everyone would be much better off if there was no political system at all – an idea known as **anarchy**. What do you think?

In the olden days – the *really* olden days – people lived in small communities that didn't have a government. They survived OK.

Maybe they *survived*, but they didn't live long and comfortable lives as we do.

But is that because we have a government? Isn't it because clever people invented things such as farming, medicine and computers?

Without a government, all those clever people would be too busy trying to find food, and keeping themselves safe, to invent things.

How do you know that for sure? I think people have always been good at looking after each other.

I think people have also been good at *killing* each other. Are you brave enough to try a big experiment?

What experiment?

Take away all governments and all laws and see what happens next...

Gulp

Thought so.

I don't even think it's true that ancient societies had no government.

A perfect world

Some thinkers, often called **political philosophers**, challenge political systems by presenting ideas they think should form the basis of a society's politics. Here are some famous examples from around the world, and across the centuries.

People need kings to set an example of how to live. If the king is virtuous, people will be virtuous.

Confucius, China, 5th century BC

Most people are stupid and selfish. An ideal system needs a strong, wise leader to keep us all in order.

Plato, Athens, 4th century BC

Government can be defined as "an institution that prevents injustice – other than the injustices it commits itself..."

Ibn Khaldun, North Africa, 14th century

People need strong governments with strict laws, otherwise we'd all murder each other.

Thomas Hobbes, England, 17th century

Even if people don't agree with all the laws of their land, they are still free, because they freely chose the overall system of law.

Jean-Jacques Rousseau, France, 18th century

The fairest way to rule is to figure out what helps the largest number of people, and do that – even if it hurts *some* people.

Jeremy Bentham, England, 19th century

People don't have rights because kings and laws say so – they all have rights, whoever they are, because they are *people*.

Thomas Paine, England/USA, 18th century

It's all very well saying "all people have rights", but in the real world we need laws to look after the rights of groups of people who are being oppressed.

Hannah Arendt, Germany/USA, 20th century

Chapter 3:
Elections and voting

Governments don't stay in power forever, even though some would like to. If there was no way to get rid of a government, it could do whatever it liked, with no consequences. In democracies, if you don't like the way a government is doing its job, you can change it by **voting** in **elections**.

Elections

In most elections, people put themselves forward as **candidates**. This is known as **standing for election**.

In some elections, the winner is put in charge of the whole country. Other elections choose candidates to be in charge of smaller local areas.

> I'm standing to be a city mayor. I have to impress thousands of people.

> That's nothing. I'm standing for election to be president and I have to make **MILLIONS** of people like me.

Candidates usually stand for election as part of a **political party** – a group with a shared set of goals or values – who compete to be in charge of the national or local government. Here are some examples of major parties around the world.

Asia

 India: Bharatiya Janata Party, Indian National Congress

 Japan: Democratic Party, Liberal Democratic Party

 South Korea: Democratic Party of Korea, Liberty Korea Party

Europe

 France: Socialist Party, Republicans, En Marche

 Germany: Social Democratic Party, Christian Democratic Union

 United Kingdom: Labour Party, Conservative Party, Liberal Democrats

Africa

 South Africa: African National Congress, Democratic Alliance

 Ghana: National Democratic Congress, New Patriotic Party

 Algeria: National Liberation Front, National Rally for Democracy

North and South America

 Argentina: Justicialist Party, Radical Civic Union

 USA: Republicans, Democrats

 Mexico: Institutional Revolutionary Party, Party of the Democratic Revolution

Some parties use symbols to represent them. For example, in the UK, the Labour Party uses a rose, the Conservative Party, a tree, and the Liberal Democrats, a bird.

Before an election, candidates, and the parties they belong to, try to persuade people to vote for them. This is called a **campaign**. Parties usually put together a list of **policies** – the things they're planning to achieve if they win.

First, candidates tell everyone their party's policies.

If we win, my party promises free healthcare for all. And we will spend more on education.

Our Policies

Candidates give interviews and go around the country talking to people.

My party promises to...

Boooooo! Get off!

(People aren't always pleased to see them.)

On election day, voters mark who they're voting for, either on paper or electronically.

Ballot paper

Ballot box

VOTE

In some elections, voters mark several candidates, putting them in order from best to worst.

Ballot Paper

2 — Purple Party
Jitan Patel

3 — Orange Party
Rachel Dobbins

1 — Red Party
Norma Fyfe

After the votes are counted, the winners are announced, and the winning candidates start their jobs as politicians. This is called **taking office**. (This sometimes doesn't happen until a few months after the elections.)

Who gets your vote?

People base their choices on all kinds of reasons. Some people base their vote on their opinion of an *individual candidate*. This could be because of what the candidate has done or promises to do... or for slightly... fuzzier reasons.

She helped my local community build a new hospital last year.

I like her policy about encouraging sport in schools.

I saw a photo of her with ketchup on her chin. I'm not voting for her.

I just think she has a kind face.

Often, people pick a *political party* and stay loyal to that party in every election. Everyone has their own reasons.

My family has always voted for the same party. It's part of who I am.

The party I vote for shares my beliefs about what's important.

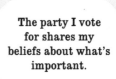

Most people where I live vote for the same party. It's traditional.

I vote for the party that looks out for me the most.

Someone who votes for different parties each time is sometimes called a **floating voter** or **swing voter**.

You might have heard the terms *left-wing* and *right-wing* used to describe politicians and parties (and people). Some parties describe *themselves* as left- or right-wing. Other people think the idea of left and right is old-fashioned.

Common left-wing ideas

People should pay lots of tax, especially rich people.

The government is the best at providing things such as healthcare and transport.

The government should make laws to protect the rights of weaker people and groups in society.

Society should change, to become fairer.

Common right-wing ideas

Taxes should be low.

Individuals and businesses are better at running their own lives than the government is.

The government shouldn't interfere too much in people's lives.

Traditional values are important and rapid social change can be harmful.

A lot of people have views somewhere in the middle – or agree with some left-wing and some right-wing ideas. And a lot of parties don't fit into these categories at all. (There's more in chapter 5 about this.)

Political parties change over time. Sometimes, if there's a big disagreement about something, they split into several new parties.

There are also **single issue** parties, which campaign about one thing, such as protecting the environment.

Who can vote? Who can't?

To vote you have to be on a list called an **electoral register**.
Most adult **citizens** can vote, and some non-citizens can too.

A **citizen** is someone born in a country, or who's become an official member of the country after living there.

I'm an adult. Can I vote in the next election?

NO Are you a citizen of the country where you live? **YES**

Is it a general (national) election?

NO →

You may be able to vote in local elections.
Are you in the military (army/navy/air force)?

YES

Sorry. Only citizens can vote in general elections in most countries. (You *may* be allowed to vote in local elections.)

NO **YES**

Depending on where you live, this might be a problem. In countries such as Egypt and Venezuela, people in the military can't vote.

YES Are you in prison? **NO**

This is because of a worry that, if soldiers get too involved in politics, they might try to take over.

Sorry. In countries such as Russia and the United Kingdom, prisoners can't vote.

Have you *ever* been in prison for a serious crime?

YES

NO

Oh dear. In some countries, such as the US, this can mean a lifetime ban on voting.

Congratulations! You can vote. Unless someone tries to stop you (see pages 64-65).

In some countries, such as Australia, if you're eligible to vote, it's against the law NOT to vote. You might have to pay a fine if you don't.

Who counts as an adult?

In most countries, you can't vote until you're *at least* 16.
Usually, the voting age is 18.

Why don't I get a vote?

Society says children are immature and don't know enough.

I know more than some adults!

Maybe, but there has to be an age limit – you wouldn't want babies voting.

Why can't the limit be something like 14? You can have a job in a lot of countries then.

Ah, but you're unlikely to earn enough to pay taxes.

Neither do unemployed adults. They can still vote.

The unemployed do other valuable things for society, though. They often raise children or look after elderly relatives.

VOTES FOR BABIES!

So, if I take grandma some tea, I can vote?

Nice try...

But, in the end, it's not in the interests of politicians to lower the voting age. Young people like changing things... including who's in charge.

Votes for (not quite) all

It's been a long struggle for many people to be allowed to vote. The right to vote is sometimes known as **suffrage**. This timeline shows which national governments were first to give the vote to women – and other groups who'd been left out of voting before.

1800s

In 19th century democracies, you had to be a property holder to vote. And you had to be a man. So only reasonably well-off men could vote.

This rule was dropped in most places during the mid-1800s. For example, in France, most men, rich or poor, could vote by 1848. (But French women had to wait almost a hundred years longer.)

1893 New Zealand

First country in the world to give all adults (including women) the vote.

1906 Finland

First country in Europe to give women the vote. Women could not only vote – they could stand for political office.

1929 Ecuador

First country in South America where women could vote.

1931 Sri Lanka
(known as Ceylon until 1972)

First country in Asia to extend voting to women. Sri Lanka was also the first country in the world to elect a female prime minister, in 1960.

Suffragettes

Women who fought for the right to vote in the 19th and 20th centuries were called **suffragettes**. They used a mixture of tactics – from chaining themselves to railings outside politicians' houses to smashing windows and planting bombs.

Women at war

During the two world wars women took on typically male jobs while the men went off to fight. This led to more support for female suffrage. **British** women got the vote in 1928, after the First World War, while in **France**, women got the vote in 1944, near the end of the Second World War.

1945 Senegal and Togo

The first countries in Africa to give women equal voting rights. But the people they were voting for were under French control, because these countries were **colonies**...

Decolonization

After the Second World War, some countries that had been previously ruled by foreign powers gained freedom. This process is known as **decolonization**.

1947 Pakistan & 1950 India

India and Pakistan were both ruled by Britain, as part of the British Indian Empire, until 1947. They then became separate, independent countries and introduced votes for women soon after that.

VOTING RIGHTS NOW!

EQUAL RIGHTS NOW!

JOBS FOR ALL!

Racism and voting rights

People from certain racial groups have historically been barred from voting in many countries – for example, black people and Native Americans in the USA. Across the world, the fight for equal votes for all people, regardless of race, has been long and hard.

1960 Canada

First Nations people in Canada – those descended from the original inhabitants – didn't get the vote until 1960.

1965 USA

In theory, black men gained the vote in the 19th century, and black women could vote from 1928, but racist laws were passed in some parts of the country to try to stop black people from voting. In 1965 the Voting Rights Act was passed, to protect black voters in all parts of the country.

1967 Australia

The country's aboriginal population (that is, people whose ancestors were from Australia and the islands around it) finally gained the vote, long after the rest of the population.

Nelson Mandela became president in the first fully democratic election in South Africa.

1994 South Africa

After the end of a racist system called **apartheid**, which gave white South Africans more rights, black people gained the right to vote in national elections.

When voting goes wrong

For most adults, voting is a simple, easy process. In some extreme cases, things get more complicated – but don't worry, problems like the ones below are fairly rare, and are illegal in most countries.

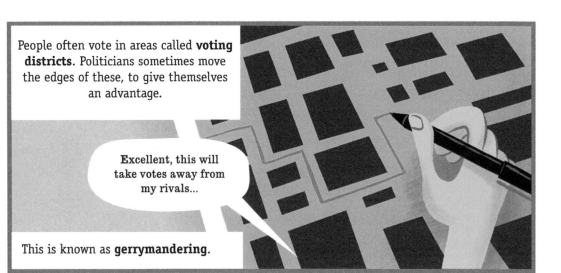

People often vote in areas called **voting districts**. Politicians sometimes move the edges of these, to give themselves an advantage.

Excellent, this will take votes away from my rivals...

This is known as **gerrymandering**.

Keeping voting safe

To make voting freer, safer and fairer, many countries have **secret ballots**, and some have **election monitors**, too:

Secret ballots

If voting is completely anonymous, and your vote doesn't have your name on it, then it's harder for people to try to bully or threaten you into voting a certain way. They will never know how you voted.

Election monitors

These are people who go to polling stations and anywhere that votes are being counted. They keep an eye on things and make sure no one's cheating. Election monitors sometimes belong to international organizations such as the Organization for Security and Cooperation in Europe (OSCE).

A watchful media

If reporters keep a sharp eye on the government, politicians and other community leaders, this can help warn people about attempts to meddle in the results of an election.

For example, in the 1970s, journalists discovered that US President Richard Nixon had spied on his rivals during an election campaign. He was forced to resign and a new election was called.

Ordinary people on social media sites can help share information about illegal or immoral election activity, too, such as voter intimidation or bribery.
Read more about the media and politics on pages 108-109.

Electoral systems

Each country has something called an **electoral system**. This is a way of working out how many elected representatives a party gets after an election, and how a government is formed. There are three main systems: **proportional representation**, **majority** and **plurality**.

Proportional representation

Proportional representation, or PR, is the most commonly-used system in national elections around the world. Each political party wins a share of available positions, usually known as **seats**, in the country's parliament or assembly, matching the share of the vote that each party has won.

> Over 90 countries use some form of PR for their national elections, including Germany, Sweden, Italy, South Africa and Japan.

> Let's say there's a national election and there are four parties competing for 500 seats. The election results turn out like this:

Blue Party — Percentage of total votes → 10%
Purple Party — 20%
Yellow Party — 30%
Peach party — 40%

Here's how 500 seats would be shared out between the parties under a PR system:

We get 50 seats. — 10%
We get 100. — 20%
150 for us. — 30%
We get 200 seats, hurrah! — 40%

In real life, it's often more complicated than that. Many countries set a minimum limit, called a **threshold**. If a party gets under, say, 5% of the votes, it won't get any seats at all. The spare seats have to be shared by the bigger parties, often using a mathematical formula.

Minority governments

If any one party has more than half the seats, they can form a government. But, under PR, it's rare for any party to manage this, meaning it's hard for one party to form a government – or at least, a government that's able to get anything done.

For example, if the Peach Party from the opposite page formed a government, the other parties could work together to stop them making a law.

A government with fewer than 50% of the seats is called a **minority government**. Minority governments don't tend to be very effective. But there's another option...

Working together

The most common type of government under PR is known as a **coalition.** That just means a government made up of representatives from two or more parties.

Parties sometimes form coalitions with other parties that they have a lot in common with.

Forming a coalition usually involves making deals and agreeing to compromise. Coalitions can happen even between parties with strong disagreements.

Plurality and majority systems

As well as PR, other electoral systems include **plurality** voting and **majority** voting. Around 80 countries use one of these systems, including the USA, Canada, the UK, France, Nigeria and India.

Plurality

Whoever gets the most votes wins, even if it's just one more than the person in second place.

Used in: UK general elections

Majority

The winner needs a majority – more than 50% – of votes. If there are more than two parties this usually means several rounds of voting.

Used in: French presidential elections

While Proportional Representation allows multiple representatives to be elected at a time, plurality and majority voting only allow one winner in each race. This is useful for when you need just one winner, such as in a presidential election.

Imagine a country is electing a president. Three candidates stand, from three parties. These are the percentages of the total votes that each wins.

In a plurality system, I become president. I have the most votes!

31% 34% 35%

This means *more than half* of citizens voted for someone other than the winning candidate.

In a majority system, I get knocked out after the first round of voting.

31% 34% 35%

In the second round, I ended up getting a lot of the blue candidate's votes... so I won!

Gah! I was doing so well!

62% 38%

But which is the best?

No electoral system is perfect, but each has strengths and weaknesses. Here are some of the arguments for and against them...

Plurality systems are best because they tend to avoid minority governments and coalitions. It's simpler for a government to make decisions if all its representatives are from the same party.

Simpler, maybe, but plurality systems are often unfair. *Most* people might end up voting for one of the losing parties, so a lot of votes are basically wasted, and only a few people get what they want.

Well, **majority** systems solve that problem. The winner always gets more than 50% of the votes. So at least 50% of voters end up getting someone they had a role in electing, even if it wasn't their first choice.

It's still not fair on people who vote for smaller parties. They never get represented! In Proportional Representation, a vote for a small party isn't automatically wasted.

That can be a good thing. Sometimes small parties hold dangerous, extreme views.

Well, large parties can have dangerous views too, especially for people in minority groups, such as immigrants*.

But it's harder to hold elected representatives to account for their dangerous views or actions under Proportional Representation, as you don't tend to vote for individual candidates, and it's harder to vote *out* politicians who do or say bad things.

Ah, but the *party* still has to hold their representatives to account. They may not even have to wait for another election!

OK, but you're leaving a lot up to the parties in your system. It's all rather complicated to understand, and comes in so many versions. In plurality and majority systems, you vote for individuals and there's only ever one winner. Simple.

*See pages 110-113

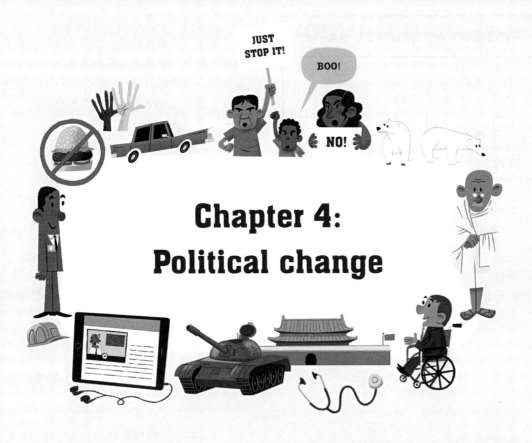

Chapter 4:
Political change

You may have to wait until the next election to vote out a government you don't like, but voting isn't the only way to bring about political change.

You can also try to change a politician's mind about a policy, or persuade them that the policy will lose them votes at the next election. There are lots of ways to do this, from writing letters to your representatives to staging a protest march.

In extreme circumstances, such as a dictatorship, people sometimes use far more drastic and less peaceful methods to bring about political change.

Putting politicians under pressure

In between elections, organizations called **pressure groups** try to persuade the government, or other representatives, to create new laws or change existing ones. Here are some types of pressure group:

Interest groups

Focus on the needs of a particular group of people. Members usually have to have a particular job or social position.

Cause groups

Focus on something that affects society as a whole. Anyone can join.

Environmental groups, such as those fighting against climate change

WWF

Greenpeace

Poverty reduction groups

Islamic Aid

Oxfam

Professional bodies (lawyers, doctors, etc)

Industrial groups, such as the tobacco industry or the car-manufacturing industry

Trade unions – groups that represent the interests of employees who work in a particular type of job, such as teachers or factory workers

Electoral reform groups, who want to change how elections work

Human rights groups, campaigning for things such as freedom of speech or the right not to be unjustly imprisoned

Amnesty International

Children's Defence Fund (CDF)

Pressure group tactics include...

- organizing protests (see page 74).
- gathering signatures in petitions.
- paying lawyers to challenge laws.
- putting out adverts to spread their message and gain more supporters.
- getting celebrities who agree with their messages to act as spokespeople.
- organizing meetings with politicians, to try to influence them directly.
- persuading the media to champion a message.

Loitering in the lobby

Trying to influence representatives about particular political issues is often called **lobbying.** The word is thought to come from the lobbies or hallways of the UK Parliament, where MPs and Lords gather and chat before debates.

Pressure groups can hire professional lobbyists to help them persuade politicians to vote in a particular way. Groups with more money to pay for lobbying are often more likely to get their voices heard, so the lobbying process isn't fair.

If a pressure group is very rich or powerful, it can be *anti-democratic*. It means the government is likely to do what small groups of people want, which isn't necessarily in the best interests of most voters.

RESIST! PROTEST!

When you think your government is doing something wrong, one way to tell them is to join a **public protest** – a gathering of people with a message that they want to get across. Here are some famous protests from the last hundred years or so.

We want voting rights and jobs!

Where and when? 1960s USA, where black people in many places had to live separately from white people, as second class citizens. A series of protests became the *Civil Rights Movement*, fighting for black rights.

Protest: The 1963 March on Washington

What happened next: The Civil Rights Movement led to the 1965 Voting Rights Act (see page 63) and other legislation to combat anti-black discrimination.

Movements

One-off protest marches rarely change anything. But when a single protest spawns *new* protests, and people form into groups to campaign for something, this is sometimes called a **movement**.

EQUALITY NOW!

JOBS AND FREEDOM FOR EVERY AMERICAN

WE MARCH FOR FREEDOM

EQUAL RIGHTS NOW!

FIRST CLASS CITIZENSHIP NOW!

CIVIL RIGHTS PLUS FULL EMPLOYMENT EQUALS FREEDOM

When a protest involves walking from one place to another, it's called a **march**.

People also protest by refusing to move from a place – for example, standing in front of bulldozers if they don't want buildings torn down.

WARNING: protests don't always end well. Sometimes, police use violence to break up protests and, in some countries, protesting itself is a crime. Some protesters become violent, too.

We want independence!

Where and when? 1930s India, which was under British rule

Protest: To protest against Britain's control of salt production, a political campaigner named Mohandas Gandhi led a march to a beach and gathered grains of salt. Collecting salt was illegal, so this was an act of **civil disobedience** – breaking the law as a protest.

What happened next? Gandhi was arrested, but soon released. Years of protests eventually helped to bring about Indian independence.

Give us democracy!

Where and when? Communist China, 1980s

Protest: In 1989, students led a pro-democracy protest in a place in Beijing called Tiananmen Square.

What happened next? The Communist government sent in tanks and many protesters were killed. China did not become a democracy although, over time, it adopted an economic system known as **capitalism**, see pages 86-87.

BLACK LIVES MATTER!

In spite of the successes of the Civil Rights Movement in the 1960s, black people still suffer from unequal treatment in the USA. The **Black Lives Matter** movement is currently campaigning about police violence against black people, and other forms of discrimination.

Revolution!

When the people of a country take power from the government, that's a **revolution**. Some use violence, while others are peaceful.

How to start a revolution

First, you need an unpopular government – almost always an undemocratic one that's hard to get rid of by other means. For example...

...**Iran**, 1970s

> Down with the Shah!

(The deeply unpopular Shah was overthrown in 1979.)

You also need an immediate crisis – or several – that whips up people's anger to a fever pitch, so that they can't bear things the way they are. For example...

...**France**, 1780s

> Bread prices are skyrocketing! The people are starving!

> Taxes are too high!

> The aristocrats and King Louis are living it up while we starve!

(The French Revolution began in 1789. King Louis XVI was executed in 1793.)

Then, you need people who are prepared to stand up to the government... and even die to bring about change.

Cuba, 1953 – revolutionary leader, Fidel Castro, led a band of rebels against the government.

> Attack, comrades!

Many of them died, or were captured and tortured. But others took up the struggle, and Castro's fighters finally beat the government in 1959.

What next?

For a revolution to succeed, it helps if the army and police decide to take the side of the revolutionaries. For example...

Tunisia, 2010-11

When people were protesting against the president, during the Tunisian revolution, the army refused orders to shoot at them.

No way!

The revolution lasted a couple more months, until the dictator-like president was removed.

Often, there's a charismatic leader who's good at persuading people to take action and put their lives at risk. For example...

Toussaint Louverture
(Haitian revolution, 1790s)

TIERRA Y LIBERTAD

Emiliano Zapata
(Mexican revolution, 1910)

Revolution!

Lenin
(Russian revolution, 1917)

People also need to know what they want to replace the old government with. Democracy? Communism? Theocracy?

After our president stepped down, a temporary government took over. By the end of 2011, we had our first free, democratic elections. I hope we'll remain a democracy.

Tunisians queuing to vote in a Presidential election in 2014

(New democracies can be fragile.)

What can I do?

As an individual, it can feel hard to know where to start to change the world. Problems such as poverty, homelessness and pollution can feel impossibly huge. But there's a lot you can do, even if you're not old enough to vote. Even just discussing politics with your friends and family can change the world, by changing people's minds.

Here are some things you could try:

Write...

...to your local political representatives and to journalists about things that matter to you, and encourage your friends to do it as well.

Join...

...a political party, a campaigning organization, such as Greenpeace, or take part in a local campaign, such as saving a local library, school or hospital.

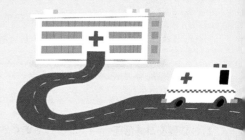

Stand...

...for election in a Youth Parliament. These are organizations that elect young people and focus specifically on issues that affect children and teenagers. They don't run countries, but governments do consult them. It's also great experience if you want to become a politician later.

Debate...

...with your friends. Schools often have debating societies, where you argue for and against an idea. Debating helps you learn to explain your ideas clearly, and how to listen and argue with people who have different ideas. Find out more on page 118.

> A vote for me is a vote to have young voices heard all over the world!

> Your argument doesn't hold together. Here's why...

> I will campaign to save our environment.

> Well, your points are based on false information.

> I promise to fight poverty if you elect me.

Pester...

...adults in your life about political issues you care about. It'll sharpen your debating skills, and you might even persuade them to change who they vote for, or to bother voting at all.

Read, watch and listen...

...to the news. In order to change the world, you need to know what's happening in it. Although, always beware of bias and try to read a variety of news sources, for balance.
Find out more on pages 108-109.

Don't buy...

...products from companies whose actions you disagree with. For example, you could avoid buying burgers from a fast food company if you know they treat their workers badly, don't pay their taxes or use child labour.

This is known as **boycotting**. If enough people boycott a company, it is more likely to change. But make sure you do your research, as a lot of accusations fly around online that aren't true.

Ask...

...questions and try to understand how your country works. The more you know, the better equipped you'll be to try to change things.

And, if you're eligible where you live:

Vote...

...in elections. It can feel as though one vote makes no difference, but every vote adds up to make a *big* difference.

Become...

...a politician. It's not a job for everyone, and it takes a lot of hard work and mental toughness. But you never know. Perhaps you're the future leader of your country?

Chapter 5:
Political ideologies

Most politicians have to make promises to get elected. For example, they pledge to make society better, or fairer. Across different parties, most politicians say they want the same thing: that everyone should have a fair chance at succeeding in life, no matter whether they were born into the richest or poorest family.

But politicians and political philosophers often have very different beliefs – or **ideologies** – about what 'succeeding' means, and about the best way to organize a society so that it really is fair to everyone.

Fixing society's problems

Politicians take on one of the hardest jobs in the world – trying to make everything better for everyone, as quickly as possible. Often, they have to try to please different groups who want – or need – very different things, and they don't have unlimited funding, either.

Why are they always funding secondary schools but leaving primary schools with nothing?

Who cares about saving for a pension? I just want to get paid more in my job.

I want to fly everywhere but I also want to protect the environment. What's the answer?

This government always puts immigrants' needs before the needs of people who were born here!

Try living in a country where you barely earn enough to feed your family and see how you like it...

If the government keeps raising tax for rich people, I'm just going to take my money and move overseas.

Being a politician is a little like being a juggler. Each ball represents an important need for society. The more balls that get added into the mix...

...the more likely it is that one will be dropped

Finding solutions

Politicians and political philosophers can try to make the world better in two very different ways.

Hello. I'm an *idealist*.

And I'm a *pragmatist*.

I don't think the world we live in is good enough. I think it could be better.

I agree! And the best way to change it is through politics.

Yes, absolutely!
Now, to start with, we need to imagine an ideal world – one that's fair to everybody.

Big waste of time! Politicians are faced with big problems that need solving *now*. That's the *pragmatic* approach.

I think that to solve any problem, you have to know what ideal end point you're working towards.

Who says what's ideal?
You?

Well, why not me?

Your ideals might not be *my* ideals.

I thought you didn't believe in ideals.

I do have *one* ideal – I think people should respect democratic decisions. Let's put our ideas to a vote, and see who wins more support!

83

Left and right, big and small

Political parties are often driven by a particular ideology that explains their policies. Often, that ideology is part of a range that people describe as stretching from left to right (see page 59).

Where do you sit?

The political terms *left* and *right* come from the 18th century. In the French National Assembly, revolutionary politicians sat on the left of the King, while his supporters sat on the right.

Who should pay for society?

The meanings of left and right have changed over time, and vary from country to country. But, roughly speaking, left-wing ideologies promote the idea that the government should intervene to help people, while right-wing ideologies believe individuals or communities are better off looking after themselves.

> I'm right-wing and I believe it's the government's job to keep people safe, but not to look after them.

> I'm left-wing, and I believe society as a whole has a responsibility to help people in bad situations.

> Why does 'society' have to mean 'government'? Can't individuals and communities help one another, without interference?

> They *could*... but I don't believe they *would*. If the government does it, via taxation, it means no one will be left out.

> But I don't think the government should *force* me to do things. And also, it'll just encourage people to wait for handouts, not to find work.

> Well, I think leaving poor people to fend for themselves gives rich people too much power!

(This discussion could continue for hours – and it often does.)

Liberals and conservatives

Left and right ideologies are often about the economy. But some people are more concerned with *cultural values*, such as laws about marriage and families, religious freedom, and what children learn in school.

I'm a **liberal**. I think it's **OK** for governments to pass laws to stop people from hurting each other. But, apart from these, governments shouldn't tell anyone how to live their life.

I'm a **conservative**. I think our society is good and worth protecting – changing too quickly is risky. A responsible government should wait until there's a clear agreement from across society before it's safe to change any law.

How big should a government be?

'Big' government doesn't mean it just has a lot of people in it. It often means the amount of money a government spends (and how much tax it asks people to pay). But it can also mean, 'how much does it interfere in people's lives?'

Big government can mean...

Lots of laws about businesses, making sure employers pay fair wages and don't rip off their customers

Laws forcing people not to take risks, for example wearing a cycle helmet

Lots of public services, such as free healthcare

Lots of police, and a secret service with the power to spy on citizens – potentially making everyone safer

High taxes

Small government can mean...

Limited power for police and spies

No laws telling people how to live their own lives, only laws ensuring people do not harm each other

Fewer laws about businesses, making it easier for new businesses to become successful quickly

Low taxes

Fewer or no public services

Capitalism and socialism

In 19th-century Europe, a change, known as the **Industrial Revolution**, swept through society. Lots of factories opened, full of machines that could produce goods very quickly, and some people started making lots of money. These changes led to the development of two new ideologies: **capitalism** and **socialism**.

Capitalists believed that the changes could only be a good thing.

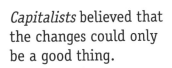

This factory is modern and efficient! We're bringing this country up to date!

But *socialists* thought that the Industrial Revolution was in fact harmful to the biggest section of society: the workers.

Factory work means long shifts...

...low pay...

...it's really boring...

...and the bosses don't care if we get hurt.

Socialists imagined a completely new way of organizing things.

Pah, take off the rose-tinted spectacles! People don't want to share. It'll never work!

We *all* own the factory together...

...we *all* work together...

...and we *all* share the results.

Some socialists tried running fair factories – but most couldn't make enough money or provide enough jobs. Extreme socialists, called commmunists, tried changing entire societies (see pages 34-35).

Socialist or capitalist? Take the test.

Start here

People should be free to earn as much money as they can, as long as they do it legally.

NO →

That's not fair! Some people will end up with lots more money!

→

You're a *pure socialist*.

Society works best when all earnings are shared.

YES ↓

Is it fair that some people get very rich while others stay poor?

NO →

Lots of rich people have an unfair advantage, such as money from their parents. Governments need to share some of that wealth.

→

YES ↑

Should governments share out all of the extra money rich people earn?

YES ↓

Most rich people deserve the money they earn, and they create jobs, too.

↓

You're a *pure capitalist*.

Society works best if people are free to make money.

NO ↓

If people can't make money from the work they do, they'll stop working very hard.

←

Governments need to give businesses room to succeed or fail. But should governments leave all businesses alone?

↓

Businesses *do* need laws, or else they may treat their staff badly.

YES ↓

Businesses *don't* need laws to force them to be kind. If they don't treat their staff well enough, they'll fail.

←

You're a *mixed capitalist*.

Businesses are more efficient than governments, but they need laws to stop them from exploiting people.

← **NO, none**

Should governments run any companies themselves, paid for by taxes?

YES, some ↓

You're a *social democrat*.

Capitalism allows businesses to run well, but isn't suitable for everything.

←

There are some things so many people rely on, it's safer for governments to have some control – such as power lines or trains.

Almost all modern democracies follow some capitalist ideals and some socialist ideals.

Nationalism

A country that is run by its own government is officially called a **state**. A **nation** is something different – it's used to mean a group of people who have a similar culture, history or language, and who feel linked to a particular place (but doesn't always describe an independent state).

Your nation is probably part of your everyday life. It's why...

...the teams you support are probably part of a national league.

One plus one is two.

...your lessons are probably in the same language as at the school down the road.

One plus one is two.

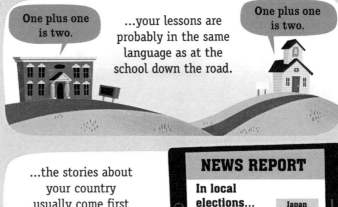

...the stories about your country usually come first on the news.

NEWS REPORT

In local elections...

Japan crisis

But which nation you belong to isn't always that clear-cut.

I live in France and I feel French, but my parents are from Brazil, so I have a Brazilian passport.

I'm a German citizen, but the sports team I support is Spanish, because I used to live there.

I live on the border of Switzerland and Italy, so I guess I'm a bit of both.

Sometimes, nations are linked to **ethnic groups**. This means groups that are – or at least, feel they are – descended from the same group of people.

Nationalism, internationalism and patriotism

Nationalists believe governments have more responsibility to help people from their own nations than people from other nations. That doesn't mean they think we have *no* responsibility towards people in other countries...

For example, if there's a flood in our country...

> The government will find new houses for everyone affected.

But if there's a flood in another country...

> The government will contribute some money to an international fund to help.

Some people believe that's unfair, and that we have an equal responsibility to help *all* human beings, no matter where they live. You could call these people **internationalists**.

> It's an accident where you're born, so you shouldn't treat people any differently.

> People in other countries can do their own thing – we should look after our own first!

> But some governments can't do a good job because their countries are poor. We should step in!

Feeling *proud* of your country or nation is known as **patriotism**. You don't have to be a nationalist to be patriotic. You might be an internationalist who thinks we should treat everyone equally, but still feel proud when you sing your national anthem.

> *Aux armes, citoyens!*
> *Formez vos bataillons,*
> *Marchons, marchons!*

Nor do you have to be patriotic to be a nationalist. You might think your country isn't anything special, but still think it's wrong to help people in other countries *before* taking care of all the people in your own country.

One state, more than one nation

Often, there is more than one nation within a single state.

For example, the United Kingdom is a state that has its own government. But within the state, there are at least four nations.

The nations are...
- Northern Ireland
- Scotland
- England
- Wales

Scottish nationalists think Scotland should become a separate state.

Northern Ireland, Scotland and Wales have their own national parliaments that run things such as health and education. But a central parliament makes decisions for the whole United Kingdom.

Some parts of the UK, such as Cornwall, are home to nationalists who want their region to be recognized as nations, too.

A new country for South Sudan

Nationalists who want to form their own independent states are known as **separatists**. There are separatist movements all over the world. In 2011, after decades of civil war, people in southern Sudan got the chance to vote on becoming independent from the rest of Sudan.

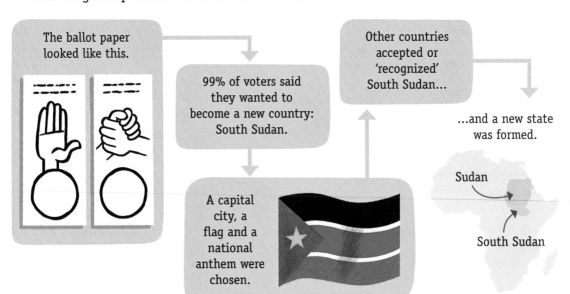

The ballot paper looked like this.

99% of voters said they wanted to become a new country: South Sudan.

Other countries accepted or 'recognized' South Sudan...

...and a new state was formed.

A capital city, a flag and a national anthem were chosen.

Sudan

South Sudan

Nationalism and violence

Yugoslavia was a group of nations that, together, formed a communist state after the Second World War. But in the early 1990s, Yugoslavia split apart into separate states. In one, Bosnia and Herzegovina, three rival nationalist parties won shares of the vote, and formed a coalition. But they all wanted different things...

We're Bosnian Muslims. We want an independent Bosnia.

The Bosnian Party of Democratic Action

We're Serbs. We want to stay part of Yugoslavia.

The Serbian Democratic Party

We're Croats*. We want to join Croatia.

The Croatian Democratic Union of Bosnia and Herzegovina

The coalition soon broke down into war. In one of the worst cases of violence, more than 8,000 Bosnian Muslims were killed by Serb forces at a town called Srebrenica†. This kind of deliberate massacre of a particular ethnic group – people who share the same culture or ancestors – is called **genocide**.

In 1995, the leaders of each group signed an agreement which ended the war and created a new system of government.

Bosnia and Herzegovina is still a single state, but has two separate parts which have quite a lot of independence.

- The Federation of Bosnia and Herzegovina – mostly Bosnian Muslims and Croats live here

- The Republika Srpska (pronounced 'serp-ska') – mostly Serbs live here

So far, this new system has been successful in preventing violence between nationalist groups.

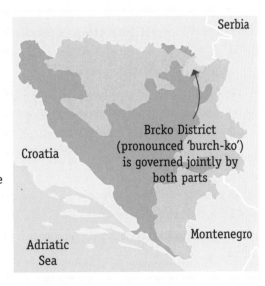

Serbia

Croatia

Brcko District (pronounced 'burch-ko') is governed jointly by both parts

Montenegro

Adriatic Sea

†Say 's-reb-ren-eats-uh'

*Say 'crow-ats'

Where do you stand?

This chart shows some examples of political ideologies, and lists a few of the ideas they promote. Most people – and most political parties – support some ideas from more than one part of the chart.

You might like some **left-wing** and some **right-wing** ideas, and prefer **big government** for some issues, but not all (see pages 85-86).

Communists

Government should provide all services, and control all industry.

Socialists

Government should provide services such as healthcare, education and electricity – and these should be paid for by taxing the rich more.

I think *I'm* in the middle!

Left wing

Shared responsibility

Social democrats

Governments should allow people to make a profit, but it should also spread out some of the country's wealth, and run some services (see page 87).

Left liberals

Governments should *make* laws to protect all people, regardless of race, gender, religion and sexuality. But they should also *reduce* laws that restrict people's choices, for example by legalizing drugs.

Left-wing anarchists

No one should be allowed to own private property, and there should be no government at all.

Left-wing libertarian

Personal property is OK, but no one should own so much of anything that they have power over other people.

Big government

Government control

Fascists

Some ethnic groups are superior to others, and the superior groups have a right to dominate the inferior ones.

Conservatives

A stable society is the most important thing. Governments should preseve a society's way of life and not change things too fast.

People in different countries often don't agree on where the political 'middle' is.

Individual responsibility

Right wing

I think *I'm* in the middle!

Classical liberals

Governments should protect all people's rights to be free, and taxes should be low – because taxation is a kind of government interference.

Capitalists

Governments shouldn't make too many rules about how people make money and run their businesses. People should buy services such as health, security and education from private companies.

Individual freedom

Right-wing anarchists

Private property is a moral right but governments should not exist.

Small government

Chapter 6:
Big questions

Political ideologies often attempt to answer a single big question: how should society work? But many people turn to politics to answer more specific and detailed questions about society.

This chapter explores just a few of those questions, from 'Can war ever be justified?' and 'What is terrorism?' to 'Is freedom of speech always a good thing?' and 'Am I a feminist?'

Is there such a thing as human rights?

Human rights are rights we *all* have *simply because we're human.*
Rights mean how a person should be treated – for example, with
kindness – and can mean things a person is entitled to have – such as
clean air to breathe. Most people agree that governments everywhere
should respect and help preserve human rights.

In 1948, the United Nations signed a document called the **Universal Declaration
of Human Rights**. Here are some of the things it said.

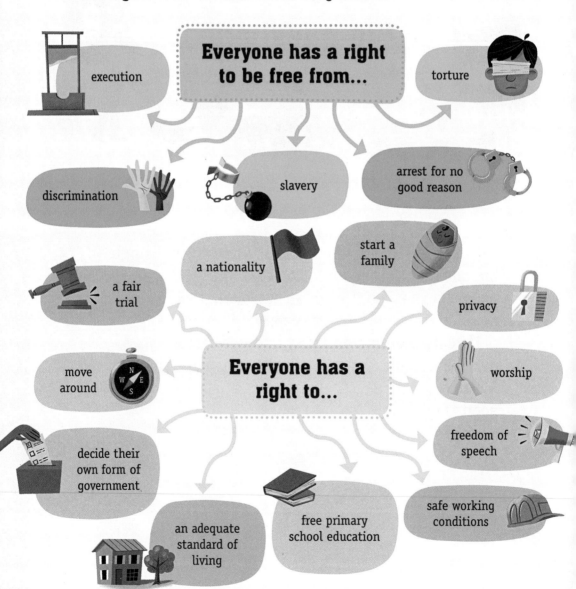

Everyone has a right to be free from...

execution

torture

discrimination

slavery

arrest for no good reason

a nationality

start a family

a fair trial

privacy

move around

Everyone has a right to...

worship

decide their own form of government

freedom of speech

an adequate standard of living

free primary school education

safe working conditions

In theory, everyone has human rights. But some people argue that theory isn't good enough. In practice, you need someone with power who will stick up for you – otherwise talking about human rights doesn't mean much at all.

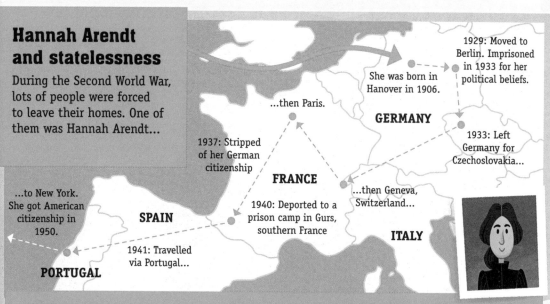

Hannah Arendt and statelessness

During the Second World War, lots of people were forced to leave their homes. One of them was Hannah Arendt...

1929: Moved to Berlin. Imprisoned in 1933 for her political beliefs.

She was born in Hanover in 1906.

...then Paris.

GERMANY

1933: Left Germany for Czechoslovakia...

1937: Stripped of her German citizenship

FRANCE

...then Geneva, Switzerland...

...to New York. She got American citizenship in 1950.

SPAIN

1940: Deported to a prison camp in Gurs, southern France

ITALY

1941: Travelled via Portugal...

PORTUGAL

Arendt described her experience as **statelessness**. She argued that what people call *human rights* are really just rights you have as a citizen of a state. If your state abandons you, there's no one else willing to defend your rights.

Today, there are still millions of stateless people. Most of them don't have the rights the Universal Declaration promises. Does this mean there *isn't* such a thing as human rights?

Talking about human rights is vital! Even if we don't manage to protect everyone's human rights all the time, we need something to aim for.

It's true that not everyone has their rights protected, but talking about human rights means that we can put bad people on trial if they abuse them.

Human rights are an impractical idea. Instead, we should try to make the world fairer, so governments can properly protect their *citizens'* rights.

How far should we be willing to go to protect human rights? Should we be willing to go to war, for example...?

Can war ever be justified?

If two people have a fight, they can be judged using their nation's laws. But when *countries* go to war, it's a matter for **international law**.

War happens when political relations between two or more countries get so bad they start using soldiers, bombs and guns. Virtually everyone agrees that war is the worst possible solution to a problem. But, on rare occasions, the UN* Security Council will agree – under terms of international law – that war *is* justified.

International law isn't all written down in one place. It's a mixture of treaties and agreements made between countries.

Why do you want to go to war?

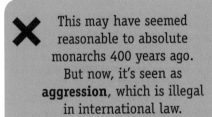

I want to get more money or more land for my country.

Another country has invaded *me*! I want to defend myself.

I think another country is getting too powerful.

I want to prevent human rights abuses in another country.

✗ This may have seemed reasonable to absolute monarchs 400 years ago. But now, it's seen as **aggression**, which is illegal in international law.

✗ Making sure no one country gets too powerful might make sense. But this is not considered a good enough justification for war by most people today.

 If another country has committed an act of aggression, it is legal (and justified) in international law to declare war to stop them.

? This is where it gets complicated. Some people think that it's not only justified, it's a *duty*. Other people think human rights can be used as an excuse for powerful countries to tell weaker countries what to do.

And it's also possible that the reason a country *claims* they've gone to war isn't the real reason at all.

*United Nations, see page 50.

Two wars in Iraq

Twice in the past 30 years, a group of countries has declared war on Iraq.

The First Iraq War

1990
Iraq invaded Kuwait. Iraq's president, Saddam Hussein, announced that Kuwait was now a province of Iraq.

IRAQ

KUWAIT

The UN demanded Iraq leave Kuwait. When Saddam refused, the UN authorized its members to go to war.

1991
Soldiers from 35 countries pushed Iraqi soldiers out of Kuwait. After just 100 hours of fighting, Iraq surrendered and the UN-backed group left.

SADDAM HUSSEIN

The UN told Saddam to pay back Kuwait for the damage done during the war, and to promise to destroy Iraq's long-range weapons.

Over ten years later, in 2002, US President George W. Bush spoke at the UN. He claimed Saddam was abusing human rights and building deadly 'weapons of mass destruction'. The UN *didn't* authorize a war. But then...

The Second Iraq War

2003
The United States – with support from three other countries – declared war on Iraq, saying they had *proof* that Saddam Hussein possessed illegal weapons.

Within days, this group of four countries captured Baghdad, the capital of Iraq, and forced Saddam to run away. Many Iraqis celebrated, because Saddam *had* been abusing human rights.

A prominent statue of Saddam Hussein in Baghdad was pulled down in 2003.

With no stable government, Iraq fell into chaos. The group stayed to help, but many Iraqis thought these outsiders had no right to interfere, and so they fought back.

2006
Saddam was captured. He was accused of human rights abuses, including genocide, and executed.

2011
All four countries finally withdrew from Iraq. Later in that year, it was discovered that Iraq had never owned the illegal weapons it was claimed.

Most people think the First Iraq War was justified. It's harder to say about the Second. Some say Saddam had violated UN rules and had abused human rights. But many suspect that the coalition wanted to get rid of Saddam because he was too powerful. And some think they *really* wanted control of Iraq's oil.

Why are some countries poor?

Although there are poor people in all countries, some countries have very high overall levels of poverty, meaning most people can't meet their basic needs. There are many causes of this, from natural disasters to problems in society and government.

Economic crisis
A country's **economy** means the amount of money, jobs and things it produces. If the economy starts to fail, a lot of people end up without jobs.

Corruption
Politicians who are **corrupt** may steal tax money. They may also run their countries badly, too. Find out more on page 115.

War
Wars can be very expensive for governments while they're happening, and rebuilding after a war costs a lot of money too.

Natural disasters
These destroy homes and businesses, instantly plunging many people into poverty.

Why are some people richer than others?

Why are some people so poor they can't afford food, when others in the same country have so much money that they can buy a wristwatch or a necklace that costs the same as a house? There are all sorts of reasons.

Money makes money
The more money you start off with in life, the easier it is to make more. So rich families become richer over the generations.

Lack of education
It's usually easier to get a well-paid job when you have lots of skills and qualifications. In many countries, education costs money, so it's harder for poor families to escape from poverty.

Luck
Some people end up in the right place at the right time to make money. For example, working for a company when it first starts to become very successful.

Some politicians think poor people could become rich if only they worked harder. Others think society needs to make people share their wealth – see the debate between capitalists and socialists on page 87.

Should rich countries help poor countries?

Rich governments often give money to the governments of other, poorer countries. This is known as **foreign aid**. But that money often comes with strings attached...

I'm from the government of a rich country.

I'm from the government of a poor country – one of your ex-colonies.

We know your country is recovering from all sorts of difficulties, not all of them your fault. We'd like to help.

Okay... that's patronising, but it'll help. We're going to spend it on a new power station. We really need a better electricity supply.

You didn't read the small print, did you? We think power stations aren't environmentally friendly, so you can't spend our money on that.

But it's our money now! Can't we decide what's best?

I'm sorry, but we just don't trust you to spend it responsibly. *We* want it spent on protecting the environment.

Hang on a minute. What about all the damage *your* government did to our environment when you were exploiting our resources?

Perhaps we shouldn't give you the money at all. Your government is corrupt, so half of it won't make it to the people who need it.

Well, maybe we don't *want* the money if it means you'll try to control how we run our lives.

What is terrorism?

Terrorism is the name for a type of violence that targets ordinary people and aims to make everyone in a society feel scared.

What do terrorists really want?

They want to make everyone afraid, so they can get their own way. They're a little like pressure groups, but they use violence and fear instead of peaceful protests.

What kinds of things do they want to make people do?

Some terrorists describe themselves as **freedom fighters**. They usually want independence for a nation that's part of another country (see pages 90-91). Other terrorists might want to change the way people live their lives, based on their beliefs.

How do people become terrorists?

Terrorist leaders often try to recruit people using a process known as **radicalization**. It involves gradually getting the person – often a teenager or student – used to extreme ideas, for example through social media, by playing on their hopes and fears.

What about extremists? What does it mean when someone's called that?

An **extremist** is someone whose views are so extreme that they will do anything to put their point across – usually including violence.

What kind of thing do extremists believe?

Some, called **fundamentalists**, base their views on twisted versions of religious beliefs. Others, for example **white supremacists**, believe that white people are superior. But there are other types, too.

How common is terrorism? Should I be scared?

Not very common at all. In most countries, far more people are killed or injured by road traffic accidents. The reason terrorist attacks make news headlines is because they're unusual.

What are governments doing to stop terrorism?

One thing most governments do is check people's bags and clothing at airports, to make sure no one brings weapons onto a plane.

So that's a good thing, right?

Checking people at airports makes it much harder for terrorists to cause harm. But it can lead to **profiling** – stopping specific groups of people more often, based on race or where they're from. Profiling is unfair.

What else are governments doing to keep us safe from terrorists?

In some countries, police have the power to arrest someone they suspect of being a terrorist, even if they don't have much proof.

That's not fair on the innocent people they arrest!

I disagree! I think that's a fair price to pay if it prevents terrorists from murdering people. I also think it's **OK** that some spy agencies are allowed to listen in on phone calls, or read private messages.

I don't want them to read mine!

It's a difficult balance. Many people think privacy is more important. But government spies and police agencies have used their powers to prevent deaths, and to arrest dangerous terrorists. I think it's worth sacrificing my privacy.

What is prison for?

In most countries, people who are convicted of serious crimes are sent to prison for years, or even for life. But taking away someone's liberty is a big step, and societies have to justify doing it.

Here are some of the main reasons societies give to justify putting people in prison.

Incapacitation

Getting criminals off the streets so they can't hurt people or commit more crimes.

Deterrence

Putting people off breaking the law, by making them scared they'll be caught and put in prison.

Rehabilitation

Making criminals less likely to commit crimes in future, by helping them and teaching them new skills in prison, so they can make money legally.

The reasons above are all practical – they either aim to prevent future crimes, or get dangerous people off the streets in the present.

Any other reasons?

There's another reason a lot of people believe in, even if they don't admit it: **retribution**. This means punishing criminals because they *deserve* to suffer for what they've done. Politicians who promise to be 'tough on crime' can appeal to people who believe in this.

A vote for me is a vote to lock up criminals!

YEAH! PUNISH THEM! MAKE THEM SUFFER!

But, taking away someone's freedom is wrong unless you're stopping something worse happening.

(Not everyone believes in retribution.)

Problems with prison

Not everyone thinks that these reasons are good enough. There are a lot of arguments about why prison doesn't work, or isn't fair.

Locking up a bunch of criminals together just means they can swap tips about how to commit crimes more sneakily in future!

Prison is very, very expensive. We should spend that money on funding *education*, to help people avoid a life of crime in the first place.

Prison sentences are racist! In the US, for instance, a black man is likely to get a 20% longer sentence than a white man for the same crime. For example, a five year sentence might turn into a six year one for a black man.

I get that prison is meant to be unpleasant but it's *really* dangerous. Too many prisoners live in fear of violence from other criminals... and even guards.

Here are some alternatives to putting criminals in prison.

Restorative justice

Getting criminals to meet their victims, apologise and do something helpful for them. This can also reduce the likelihood of someone commiting another crime.

Retraining

Taking a class can help some criminals learn to change their ways – for example, driving courses for speeders or drunk-drivers.

Monitoring

Wearing an electronic tag that allows the police to track where criminals go, so they can't get up to too much trouble...
...in theory.

Community service

Doing work that makes life better for people, such as picking up litter and removing graffiti.

105

What is freedom of speech?

Freedom of speech – also known as **freedom of expression** – is the idea that people should be able to share their ideas without fear of being arrested.

When a government or another powerful group limits someone's freedom of speech, it's called **censorship**. This might mean banning certain books, or stopping people who are considered dangerous from speaking in public places.

The word *censor* comes from the name of a government official in Ancient Rome whose job included keeping an eye on how Roman citizens behaved.

Neglecting your fields? That's positively *unroman*. You're in trouble now!

A Roman *censor*

Why do we need freedom of speech in politics?

Being free to share information – and ideas – allows voters to make decisions based on what's *really* going on. If people aren't able to report the facts, especially those that expose a government's failings, democracy won't work properly. That's why dictators love censorship.

Don't believe those dangerous lies! **TAKE HER AWAY!!!**

Anyone else care to comment?

Our leader has arrested my family. I don't know where he's taken them.

We think you're **GREAT**, sir...

Squashing free speech means dictators can tell people that everything is fine, even when they're committing terrible crimes – and no one is able to say otherwise. Using strict censorship also scares people from daring to speak up against the government.

Is freedom of speech always a good thing?

On the whole, freedom of speech is good for democracy. But many think there should be *some* limits to what you're allowed to say – or write, or sing – in public. Still, not everyone agrees on where society should draw the line.

Freedom of speech means I should be allowed to say anything I like!

Even if what you say puts someone in danger?

How can *words* put someone in danger?

Let's say you know where a team of soldiers are hiding. Should you be free to post that online and probably get them killed?

OK, maybe I shouldn't be allowed to post *that* kind of thing. But apart from that, I should be able to say what I want.

What about... if you go on **TV** and tell viewers to go out and kill people? Should that be against the law?

It depends... what if I say it as a joke? I'm not comfortable with the government or lawyers deciding what's funny...

OK, jokes are a tricky one. What if I wanted to say something horrible, such as 'All gay people are evil'? Some people call that *hate speech*.

Where do you draw the line on that, though? Are you going to start banning all opinions you disagree with?

What about if you spread harmful lies about someone? Should that be illegal?

It depends on the lie.

You like saying 'it depends', don't you? Has anyone ever told you you should go into politics?

How does the media affect politics?

The media is shorthand for the way people share information – TV news, the internet, print newspapers and magazines. In totalitarian political systems, the government controls the media but, in a democracy, a healthy, independent media is vital.

But there is also a darker side to the relationship between the media and politics, even in a democracy...

The good

The media can...

- dig up the truth and uncover secrets that politicians would rather bury, and let everyone know what the government is up to.

- help to keep citizens informed about politics – which laws are being passed, what's being debated, and where the country is heading.

- ask politicians challenging questions, giving the public a chance to see how they perform under pressure, and whether their ideas make sense when you look at them carefully.

- publish campaign promises during elections so people can make informed voting decisions.

- offer historical context: when something big is happening in politics, it's often similar to something that's happened before. The media can bring on experts who can draw historical parallels and help us understand the present.

The bad

The media can also...

- report the news in a **sensationalist** way. For example, making out political news stories to be more extreme than they actually are.

- show strong **bias** towards one party or set of beliefs. If the people who run a particular news site hold strong political beliefs this will affect which news stories they cover, and how they cover them.

- be corrupt. Journalists, broadcasters or newspapers might take bribes in order to report things in a way that puts a certain politician in a good or bad light. (Luckily, other journalists can work to uncover this corruption.)

- be influenced by their bosses, who pay their wages – even if they're not actually corrupt. Many news companies are owned by individual billionaires, who have strong biases, or something to gain from helping or harming certain political parties.

- allow extreme views to take hold. If an extremist is given enough airtime, people can start to think that person's views are OK.

What can you do?

As a reader and viewer, the best thing to do is to read and watch a wide variety of news sources, and to read beyond the shouty headlines. Ask yourself if the news source you're using is trying to get you to react in a certain way, by using emotional language instead of facts.

What is immigration?

People who choose to move to another country are usually called **immigrants**. There are many reasons to do this, from wanting better weather, to needing better job opportunities. People who leave their countries to escape wars or other dangers are known as **refugees**. Unlike immigrants, refugees don't really have a choice.

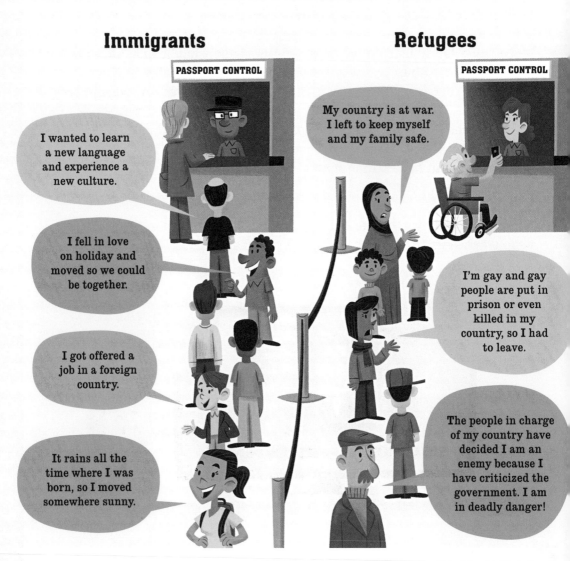

Most countries have strict rules about who they will let in as immigrants. Often, newcomers to a country have fewer rights, such as not being able to vote, or not being allowed to see a doctor for free. Refugees often have to work very hard to prove they are genuinely in danger, too. Even then, they may only be allowed to live in camps, not in proper homes.

Why are people against immigration?

Some political parties win votes by whipping up fears about the effects of immigration in their country, such as the idea that immigrants are 'stealing' jobs from locals. Some politicians also tap into a distrust of foreigners, known as **xenophobia.** Many of these fears aren't based on reality, but it's hard to persuade someone to change their feelings using logical arguments.

Immigrants are stealing our jobs!

Many immigrants only come to the country *because* they've been offered a job – a job no one in the country wanted.

Well, immigrants will drive down wages then, because they're willing to work for less.

Not if the government makes it illegal to pay low wages.

I don't feel like I'm at home in my own country any more. Immigrants don't know how our society works, and some don't share our values.

I think having immigrants from around the world has made our society better – especially the food! And remember, immigrants learn from our culture, too. A confident, peaceful society should be able to pass on its values, as well as learning new ones.

That sounds nice in theory, but it's not what I see happening around me. I was happy with the way things were.

Living with racism

Racism is a belief that some races are superior to others. People who hold racist views are likely to treat people of other races badly. You don't have to be an immigrant to experience racism – your family could have lived in a country for centuries and still be a victim of racist insults, and worse.

Most governments have laws to protect people from racism, such as not giving people jobs based on what they look like, or because their names sound 'foreign'. But it's very hard to create laws to prevent more subtle forms of racism.

Am I a feminist?

Human rights apply to everyone. But some groups, even very large ones, have often lived at a big disadvantage. For example, women and girls haven't always had the same rights as men and boys, and in lots of ways still don't.

Here are some of the questions that women often have to worry about more than men and boys – often depending on the part of the world in which they live.

People who recognize that women and girls are treated unfairly, and believe they should have equal rights and opportunities to men and boys, are known as **feminists.** If you believe that, you're a feminist, too – even if you're not a woman.

Is under-representation a problem?

When people from minority groups aren't seen or heard, it's called **under-representation**. For example, in Hollywood movies roughly 70% of all speaking parts go to men (usually white men).

In most parliaments around the world, there are far more male than female representatives. Under-representation in government often affects other groups of people, too, such as gay people, disabled people and ethnic minorities.

But is it a problem?

No! Representatives have to care for *everyone*, especially if they want to get re-elected. Female voters will get rid of a male representative if he's sexist!

Yes! It's impossible to understand what it's like to be part of a minority unless you've experienced it yourself.

Yes! If people from minorities don't see anyone like them in parliament, they won't think that the top jobs are for them.

No! If there aren't many women politicians today, it's a sign that women just don't want to go into politics. You can't force them!

Yes! Parties have a responsibility to choose candidates from minorities. Otherwise, nothing will ever change.

Maybe... but most people don't actually care much about parliament. It's real-life things – such as equal wages – that make the *real* difference.

Who's responsible for the planet?

Humans have done terrible things to planet Earth, from dumping oil and pumping out pollution to causing climate change by burning fossil fuels. Most people agree society needs to fix this – but how can politicians help us protect the environment?

Politicians can make laws to reduce pollution and tackle climate change. For example, they could ban cars that burn fossil fuels, or at least raise taxes on them.

Ah, but politicians don't all **WANT** to make laws like that because lots of voters can't afford new cars, or they want to make money out of fossil fuels.

But there are lots of politicians who **DO** want to help. And, unlike us, they have access to scientists and other experts, who can advise them on how society as a whole needs to change, if we want to save our planet.

What about the fact that governments change every few years, and the next government could undo any laws the previous one made?

Good point. So maybe it's more important to lobby private companies, instead of government?

You don't even have to lobby a company to make it change. If enough customers simply stop buying their products it's a very powerful motive for a company to change its ways.

But shouldn't government work to encourage companies to change, rather than relying on people to protest?

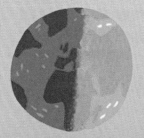

That's a nice idea in theory. But governments are made up of people, and people can become corrupt. The news is full of stories about government officials being friends with companies that create pollution...

Is corruption inevitable?

Corruption happens when politicians use their positions in dishonest ways, to gain money or power. Corruption could be any of the following things.

Bribery
Agreeing to give someone special treatment in return for money

Extortion
Using threats or violence to get ahead in politics

Nepotism
Giving money or important jobs to friends and family

Blackmail
Using other politicians' secrets against them

Embezzlement
Stealing money that's supposed to belong to the government

Here's one example.

DAILY NEWS   LOCAL NEWS   WORLD NEWS   SPORT   WEATHER

SCANDAL IN BRAZIL

In 2014, Brazilian police launched an investigation into corruption. It was revealed that companies who had been paid government money for big construction projects were using part of it to bribe government officials. Billions of dollars were ending up in the pockets of politicians.

For the next two years, there were anti-corruption protests across Brazil. People carried yellow and green brooms, demanding that politicians stop stealing money that they had paid in taxes.

In 2016, President Dilma Rousseff was sacked. Many company bosses and politicians were arrested and had to pay enormous fines.

CLEAN UP YOUR ACT!

▶ Protesters demand an end to corruption

How to argue

In life, you're likely to come across a lot of people you disagree with. Here are some tips for how to create a convincing argument... without hurting people's feelings.

❶ Don't make it personal

Pick apart someone's *ideas* rather than saying anything about them as a person.

❷ Back up your opinions with facts

To find the facts in the first place, read and watch the news, and read widely around subjects you care about.

❸ Appeal to people's emotions

Although facts are important, humans are emotional creatures, so if you can tap into someone's fears and hopes, you're more likely to persuade them. Often, people need to have a personal connection to an argument – sometimes facts alone can feel cold and abstract.

So, why should I care if the school has sacked four teachers?

Because the teachers who are still here will be overworked and might shout at you a lot.

4 Look out for arguments built on lies

Sometimes, someone might be using a piece of false information as the starting point for their argument. For example...

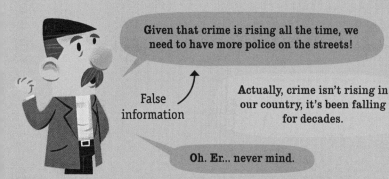

Given that crime is rising all the time, we need to have more police on the streets!

False information

Actually, crime isn't rising in our country, it's been falling for decades.

Oh. Er... never mind.

It's important to challenge any assumptions your opponent is making at the start, so they can't create an argument based on incorrect or out-of-date facts.

5 Don't lose your temper and shout

It's rude and disrespectful, and it will also make your arguments seem weaker, as you look like you're panicking and losing control.

RAAAAGE RAAANNNT

Woah, calm down!

✗

I care about the issue but my voice is level.

He seems reasonable.

✓

Speaking passionately is fine; just don't yell.

6 Be prepared to change your mind

Sometimes, you might realize halfway through an argument that the other person might be right. That's OK. You don't have to keep arguing for the sake of it. Being honest about changing your mind can help others change their minds, too.

...and that's why I think the voting age should be lowered to 16.

Hmm... I've never thought of it like that before.

Learn to debate

One good way to learn how to have (and win) political arguments is to join a **debating society**. Schools and colleges often have these. In debates, people have arguments, following strict rules, and the audience votes on who wins.

Here's how a debate works...

Someone called the speaker reads out the suggestion – or **motion** – that's going to be debated.

This house believes that school bullies should be arrested by the police.

The **proposer** presents an argument agreeing with the motion. She or he has few minutes to speak.

Then, the **opposer** speaks against the motion, with the same time limit.

The harm caused by bullying in schools is just as great as that caused by muggers.

If we make nasty behaviour illegal, where do we stop? Do we make it illegal to snap at someone when you're angry?

Other people speak to back up both sides, then, after a summing up, the audience votes.

The votes have been counted. The blue team wins!

Who won?

☒ Blue
☐ Green

Many parliaments around the world use similar rules to debate before voting on a bill. So debating is very good training for a career in politics.

Some debates are about serious topics:

- should the death penalty exist?
- should we lower the voting age to 16?
- does social media make you more antisocial?

...but people practise using silly topics, too:

- who would win in a fight between a vampire and a werewolf?

What next?

Once you've finished this book, you'll probably know more about politics than the average person. But don't stop there. The world of politics is always changing. Watch and read the news to learn more.

Read about history. Spanish-American philosopher George Santayana wrote in his book *The Life of Reason*: "Those who cannot remember the past are condemned to repeat it." The more you know about political history, the readier you'll be to stop bad things from happening in the future.

Keep your eyes, ears and mind open. Ask yourself what you believe. Question those beliefs. Never passively accept what someone tells you. Vote, when you're old enough. Protest, if you disagree with your government. Write letters and emails to your representatives.

And even, perhaps, become a politician yourself...

Glossary

This glossary explains some of the words used in this book.
Words written in *italic* type are explained in other entries.

absolutism a *political system* in which one person, such as a *monarch* or *dictator*, runs the country, with total control over everything.

anarchy when no one is in charge, or when there is no *government* at all.

authoritarianism a *political system* in which *government* has strict control, for example by outlawing freedom of speech.

ballot an *election* in which people vote, often using pieces of paper called ballots.

bias when the *media* or a *politician* discusses an issue from just one point of view.

cabinet a group of senior *politicians*, usually chosen by a *president* or *prime minister* to help run the government.

candidate a person who puts themselves forward to be elected as a *politician*.

capitalism an *ideology* that says the *economy* works best if people are free to set up businesses without too much interference from *government*.

censorship when a *government* tells people what they can and can't write or even say.

central government *government* that has authority over an entire country, usually based in the capital city.

citizen a person who is part of a *state*, often the state they were born in. Most adult citizens can vote and be *candidates*, and have to pay *taxes*.

civil servant someone who works for the *government* but is not elected. In many countries, civil servants have to be politically neutral.

coalition when two or more *political parties* work together to form a *government*.

colony a country ruled over by a *government* from another country.

communism a *left-wing political system* based around the idea that everyone should share resources equally, organized by a powerful *central government*.

constitution a set of rules, often written down, that outlines the basic *political system* of a *state*.

corruption when *politicians* use

their position of power to get money or or advantages for themselves.

debate a way to discuss competing ideas, often used in *parliaments*.

democracy a *political system* in which *citizens* can elect a new *government* every few years.

dictator the leader in an *authoritarian* system.

direct democracy a *political system* in which *citizens* are asked to vote on new laws as well as to elect *governments*.

economy the way that money moves in and around a *society*, and how a *government* manages that movement.

election when *citizens* all vote on who should be their new leader, or who should be in their next *government*.

empire a country that has conquered or taken over running other countries.

executive branch the part of *government* that approves new laws and is responsible for carrying out *policy* ideas.

federal republic a *state* made up of a group of smaller regions (often also called states), ruled by an elected leader.

feminism the belief that women and men should have equal rights and opportunities.

freedom of speech the right for people to say and write and share any ideas without fear of *censorship* or arrest.

government a group of people that run a country, often split across three branches: *executive*, *legislative* and *judicial*.

green politics *policies* or *protest movements* based around controlling human impact on the environment.

human rights basic things that all people should have acccess to, such as food, shelter and freedom from being harmed by others.

ideology the basis for a way of thinking about *society*, or a *political system*.

immigration when people who are originally *citizens* of one country, or no country, move countries.

independence being free from control by other people, organizations or countries.

international organization a collection of countries working together with a shared aim, for example the United Nations.

judicial branch part of a *government* responsible for deciding how to interpret laws, and who has broken them.

left-wing a broad *ideology*, usually defined by the belief that *governments* should impose high *taxes* and share resources between all *citizens*.

legislative branch part of a *government* responsible for discussing and agreeing on new laws and *policies*.

liberalism an *ideology* roughly defined by the belief that *governments* should not tell people how to live their lives, and should not spy on them.

local government governments within a country that are responsible for a small part of that country, such as a city.

majority the largest group of people in a country, or what a *political party* has if it has more than half of the representatives in a *parliament*.

media, the websites, TV shows, newspapers and any other way journalists and *politicians* talk to people in a *society*.

minority any group of people in a *society* who are fewer than the *majority* group – often at risk of

being mistreated by that group.

monarchy a country ruled by a king, queen or emperor.

nationalism an *ideology* based on doing what is best for the people within a particular country or *state*.

parliament where *politicians* meet to debate *policies* and make laws. In some countries, it's called a congress, or an assembly.

patriotism an *ideology* based around feeling strong pride for your own country or *state*.

policy a specific idea a *government* carries out to improve *society*, such as an 'education policy'.

political party a group of people with a shared *ideology*, who try to get their *candidates* elected to a national *parliament*.

political system a set of rules that defines who can form a *government*, and what powers that government has.

politician someone who has been elected to their national *parliament*, and is able to *debate* and vote directly on new laws and *policies*.

president the leader of a *republic*. In some countries, a president is the most powerful politician; in others, her or his power is mostly ceremonial.

pressure group people who work together to try to influence *politicians*, for example by organizing a *protest movement*.

prime minister the leader of the *government* in some countries, usually in charge of the *legislative branch*.

protest movement a series of actions, such as marching or letter writing, to try to persuade a *government* to change the law.

public services things a *government* provides for its *citizens*, such as street lighting.

referendum a vote to answer a specific question, rather than an *election*.

representative democracy a *political system* in which *citizens* regularly elect *politicians* to represent their views in a *parliament*.

republic a country that does not have a monarchy, but is ruled by *politicians*.

right-wing a broad *ideology*, usually defined by the belief that traditional values should be upheld, and that *citizens*, not *governments*, are responsible for their own welfare.

socialism an *ideology* that promotes the idea that *society* can overcome inequality by letting *government* control services, such as education and healthcare, and using *taxes* to spread out wealth.

society a group of people, usually with shared values and aims. It can be small, such as a family, or large, such as a country.

state a country or collection of countries ruled by a single central government, often united by a shared culture and language.

suffrage the right to vote, usually applied to national elections.

suffragettes women who campaigned for the right to vote in the 19th and 20th centuries.

taxes money that *citizens* and businesses must pay the *government*, to be spent on running the country.

terrorist someone who performs acts of violence, often without warning and at random, to try to scare a *society*.

totalitarianism an extreme version of *authoritarianism*, in which a leader often demands that *citizens* worship them and obey direct commands.

treaty an official agreement between governments from two or more countries.

Index

EU, the, 51
executive, 40-41, 44

fascism, 33, 93
federal republics, 49
feminism, 112, 113
feudalism, 21, 30
foreign aid, 101
foreign policy, 6
Founding Fathers, the, 25
France, 10, 36, 62, 76
freedom fighters, 102
freedom of speech, 106-107
fundamentalists, 102

Gandhi, Mohandas, 75
genocide, 91
gerrymandering, 65
government, 10-11, 40-49, 84-85

Hobbes, Thomas, 53
House of Representatives, the,
    25, 42
human rights, 96-97

Ibn Khaldun, 53
idealists, 83
ideology, 81, 84-85, 92-93
idiots, 15
immigration, 110-111
India, 49, 63, 75
international organizations,
    50-51
Iran, 33, 76
Iraq, 99
Italy, 33

judges, 40, 43
judicial, 40-41

kings, 10, 21

laws, 7, 40-44, 46
left-wing, 59, 84, 92
legislative, 40-41, 44
legitimate government, 11
Lenin, 34, 35, 77
liberals, 85, 92-93
lobbying, 73
local government, 48, 49
Louis XIV, 22-23

majority, 39
majority voting system, 68-69
Mandela, Nelson, 63
marches, 74-75, 78
Marx, Karl, 34-35
media, the, 38, 65, 78, 79, 106,
    108-109
meritocracy, 20
military junta, 33
ministers, 44, 45, 46
minority governments, 67
monarchy, 22-23, 44
MPs, 38, 44-45

nation, 88-91
nationalism, 88-91
Native Americans, 25, 63
NATO, 51
nepotism, 20, 115
news, 108-109
Nixon, Richard, 65

125

Usborne Quicklinks

For links to websites where you can find out more about politics, governments, elections and voting with videos, virtual tours, activities and quizzes, go to the Usborne Quicklinks website at

www.usborne.com/quicklinks

and type in the title of this book. Please follow the internet safety guidelines at the Usborne Quicklinks website.

Always beware of bias

Here are some of the things you can do at Usborne Quicklinks:

- See inside the House of Commons in the UK
- Explore the similarities and differences between the UK Prime Minister and the US President
- Take a virtual tour of the White House in the US
- Find facts about political systems in India, Japan and other countries
- Discover leaders of every country in the world from ancient times to present day

Acknowledgements

Written by
Alex Frith, Rosie Hore
& Louie Stowell

Illustrated by
Kellan Stover

Designed by Jamie Ball &
Freya Harrison

Series designer:
Stephen Moncrieff
Series editor:
Jane Chisholm

Politics experts:
Dr. Hugo Drochon,
University of Cambridge
and Dr. Daniel Viehoff,
New York University

With thanks to:
Lupita Harris, John Pienaar,
Rachel Reeves MP, Nick Clegg MP
and The Earl Howe, PC

First published in 2017 by Usborne Publishing Ltd., Usborne House,
83–85 Saffron Hill, London, EC1N 8RT, United Kingdom.
www.usborne.com